PARACHUTE GAMES

Todd Strong, MS
Dale LeFevre, MA

D0451172

Human Kinetics

Library of Congress Cataloging-in-Publication Data

Strong, Todd.
    Parachute games / Todd Strong, Dale LeFevre.
      p.   cm.
    ISBN 0-87322-793-X
    1. Parachute games. 2. Physical education and training.
  I. Lefevre, Dale. II. Title.
GV1218.P34S77 1996
793--dc20   95-24027
                                              CIP
ISBN: 0-87322-793-X

Copyright © 1996 by Todd Strong and Dale LeFevre

All rights reserved. Except for use in a review, the reproduction or utilization of this work in any form or by any electronic, mechanical, or other means, now known or hereafter invented, including xerography, photocopying, and recording, and in any information storage and retrieval system, is forbidden without the written permission of the publisher.

Notice: Permission to reproduce the Games Finder on pages 44-46 in this book is granted to those who have purchased *Parachute Games*. The reproduction of other parts of this book is expressly forbidden by the above copyright notice. Persons or agencies who have not purchased *Parachute Games* may not reproduce any material from this book.

Acquisitions Editors: Rick Frey, PhD; Scott Wikgren; **Developmental Editors:** Mary E. Fowler, Elaine Mustain; **Assistant Editor:** Erin Cler; **Editorial Assistants:** Andrew Starr, Amy Carnes; **Copyeditor:** June Waldman; **Proofreader:** Karen Bojda; **Typesetting and Layout:** Ruby Zimmerman; **Text Designer:** Judy Henderson; **Photo Editor:** Boyd LaFoon; **Cover Designer:** Jack Davis; **Photographer (cover and interior):** Marion Crombie; **Printer:** United Graphics

Human Kinetics books are available at special discounts for bulk purchase. Special editions or book excerpts can also be created to specification. For details, contact the Special Sales Manager at Human Kinetics.

Printed in the United States of America   10

Human Kinetics
Web site: www.humankinetics.com

United States: Human Kinetics
P.O. Box 5076
Champaign, IL 61825-5076
800-747-4457
e-mail: humank@hkusa.com

Canada: Human Kinetics
475 Devonshire Road, Unit 100
Windsor, ON N8Y 2L5
800-465-7301 (in Canada only)
e-mail: orders@hkcanada.com

Europe: Human Kinetics
107 Bradford Road
Stanningley
Leeds LS28 6AT, United Kingdom
+44 (0)113 255 5665
e-mail: hk@hkeurope.com

Australia: Human Kinetics
57A Price Avenue
Lower Mitcham, South Australia 5062
08 8277 1555
e-mail: liahka@senet.com.au

New Zealand: Human Kinetics
P.O. Box 105-231, Auckland Central
09-523-3462
e-mail: hkp@ihug.co.nz

Contents

To Larry Diamond who first taught us
to play with parachutes

Acknowledgments

Thank you to all the friends, family, and others who participated in the photo sessions. Particularly, thank you to the Mendocino Elementary School (CA); Fort Bragg Middle School (CA); East Oxford First School (UK); East Oxford Woodcraft Folk (UK); Cardinal Newman Middle School (UK); and Playschemes at Blackbird Leys, Temple Cowley, and Rosehill (UK).

#

It's time to revive those under-used parachutes bundled away in storage. If you're a teacher or recreation professional looking to enliven your group's physical activity program, *Parachute Games* will inspire you to unpack the old parachute and bring it back to life. If you've never played with parachutes, you'll want to buy one today and introduce this exciting new activity to your players.

Whether you're a novice or already a parachute aficionado, *Parachute Games* will

- add to the number of games you already know,
- give you ways to categorize games for different play groups and settings,
- provide advice on how to present the games,
- group games by developmental skill, and
- show you how to care for and maintain your parachute.

The idea for this book came while watching a group of elementary school children play with a parachute during their physical education class. Watching the kids and teachers having so much fun reminded us of all the great parachute games and activities we have learned, played, and shared. So, we decided to put our experience and enthusiasm into a book. This book is our way of sharing our excitement with you.

This book has two parts. In Part I we include everything you need to make parachute games exciting, instructional, and safe in a variety of settings. In chapter 1 we look at the benefits of parachute play and suggest low-cost items that can complement your activities. In chapter 2 you'll find useful tips on how to lead the games so you can add to the playfulness while you explain the rules. We'll help you become aware of different play leadership styles and techniques and show you the best way to present the games.

Chapter 3 lists games by skills needed to play them to recognize the close association between enhancing developmental skills and the learning process. To ensure that you get full value from the equipment, chapter 4 identifies features to look for when you buy a parachute, including a list of sources. We also recommend the best ways to store your parachute and give tips on how to maintain and mend it so it will last.

In Part II you'll find a comprehensive list of our favorite parachute games. We bring these to life using photographs to illustrate our explanations and descriptions. We precede chapter 5 with three sample play sessions to pique players' interest. Then, we divide the games into categories—low activity in chapter 5, moderate activity in chapter 6, and high activity in chapter 7—and present them in alphabetical order. A handy Games Finder will help you quickly identify which games will fit your immediate needs.

The format in which each game is presented in chapters 5 through 7 will help you figure out your personal list of great parachute games. We share tips on what games work well in specific settings, such as the type of surface the parachute will be used on. We consider the age, size, number, and diversity of the players plus items such as intensity level of the game to help you choose appropriate games. Finally, we present interesting sequences of games that work well together to help you design a fun, meaningful play session no matter where or with whom you are playing.

We hope that sharing our experience and enthusiasm in this book allows more and more people to play. Please enjoy; and have as much fun using this book as we had in researching and writing it.

Understanding Parachute Play

The word *parachute*—which comes from the French *parare*, to protect, and *chute*, fall—can be translated literally as "protecting from a fall." Although Leonardo da Vinci had already sketched an early parachute model by 1495, it was not until the late 18th century that people began using parachutes to drop safely from the sky. Jean Blanchard, a noted balloonist of the period, amused audiences by dropping animals attached to parachutes from his air-borne balloon. Andre Garnerin was braver: On October 22, 1797, he cut himself from a balloon and safely descended some 3,000 feet to the ground in the first successful parachute drop involving a human. Polish aviator Jodaki Kuparaento first used a parachute as an emergency life-saving device, jumping on July 24, 1808, from a balloon that was on fire. Since then parachutes have saved thousands of lives.

As parachute designs improved, the new sport of skydiving became ever more popular. By 1936 skydivers were competing with one another, jumping out of planes and flying free for thousands of feet before opening their parachutes. Thanks to improved designs, parachutists now have maneuverability and accuracy that was unthinkable in the sport's early days.

Whoever first thought of using a parachute as a giant game piece remains anonymous. When relatively inexpensive used parachutes appeared in army surplus stores in the 1960s, pioneers found the opportunity and inspiration to create new recreational and physical education activities. Larry Diamond, in particular, amazed us in the early 1970s by his giant parachute wizardry at New Games festivals in the Bay Area of San Francisco.

Today parachute makers design and build colorful play equipment specifically for people to enjoy together on the ground—and we hope you will use *Parachute Games* to do just that.

Discovering the Benefits of Parachute Play

When the first daredevils used parachutes to float safely down to earth they probably had no idea of the advances that were to come. Today's parachutes allow for control that was unheard of in the beginning days of parachuting. Those early parachute jumpers also could not have imagined how much fun a group of people could have playing with a parachute while staying on the ground. This chapter presents some of the benefits of playing with a parachute.

Parachute Play Promotes Cooperation

Playing with a parachute promotes teamwork and cooperation. When playing with a parachute everyone shares the same piece of equipment at the same time. In sports such as football, basketball, or volleyball, the players use the same piece of equipment (i.e., a ball); but rather than sharing it, they compete to control it. In parachute play, instead of fighting over who dominates the equipment, all the players are in contact with a parachute and work together toward a creative end. Even when teams are playing against each other, as in the game of Popovers, people still share the parachute. This gives a more cooperative feel to the game than if people are always fighting over who has control of the equipment.

Because play parachutes are round, the players naturally form into a circle around the edge. Being in a circle lets all the players see each other. This visual contact creates a group awareness that contributes to people playing more cooperatively and safely.

In contrast, imagine the same group of people playing with an Earthball. An Earthball is an inflated ball 6 feet in diameter, painted to look like the earth. In most Earthball games each player focuses on the ball rather than on the other players. An Earthball is so big that players on opposite sides often cannot see each other. The excitement of playing with such a large ball combined with the absence of awareness of other players means that people could get run over if no one were supervising. Parachutes share the same bigger-than-life quality of an Earthball, but are inherently safer. The circular formation around a parachute forces people to be aware of and cooperate with the group.

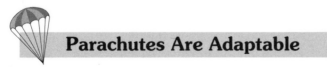

Everybody Wins

There are no losers in parachute games. Many parachute games involve no competition at all. Parachute activities often consist of everyone playing together to achieve a shared goal. Some of the games, however, are competitive. Many of these competitive games involve the entire group playing together on the same team and competing with itself. For example, the World Record Merry-Go-Round game involves competition, but the team is trying to beat its own previous record.

Even in games that involve competition between different teams, the focus is on playing. Each round lasts for only a short time, and there is no stopping between rounds to award points or hand out medals. The players are having so much fun they want to get on to the next round or the next game. No one worries about winning or losing.

Parachutes Are Adaptable

Parachute games are flexible. You can play with a parachute for 5 minutes or for an hour. Because parachutes are easy to unpack and store, you won't waste time in setting up or taking down the equipment.

Parachute games encompass a wide range of activity levels. Parachutes work well for noisy, physical games or for quiet ones.

The smallest group of people we have ever seen play together with a parachute is two. A large parachute starts to become crowded at around 40 players.

One important characteristic of parachute games is that players of different abilities, sizes, and ages can play together. This means parachute games are perfect for families and at events such as community festivals where everyone is invited to play. Parachute games also work well in coeducational physical education classes. At Special Olympics events the spectators can play right along with the Olympians.

Parachute Play Is Creative

Parachutes lend themselves to imagination. The chance to play with a 30-foot diameter swatch of fabric does not come often to most people. This rare sight triggers our creative senses. As a result we are ready to become alligators, treasure hunters, cats, robbers, or other characters. In addition, this huge, billowing fabric can turn into a cloud, swamp, ocean, or igloo.

The Leader Can Play, Too

One of the great things about parachute games is that the leader also gets a chance to play. In many other types of games the leader is more of an authority figure and must remain outside the game to act as a referee. The rules and the outcomes of these other games take on such importance that people feel better if a nonplayer watches to decide if the game is being played correctly. Because we don't keep score in parachute games, no one has to worry about who won or whether the game is being played strictly by the rules.

Behavioral problems that might be amplified by a teacher's position of authority are diffused when that interaction changes into just two players talking to each other. Some teachers have told us that this

new role of fellow player allowed them an opportunity to relate to some problem students in a new, more positive way. They were able to carry this new style of interaction beyond the play session and make some improvements in their overall teacher-student relationships.

Parachutes Are Cost Effective

Considering the potential number and diversity of players that can participate in and enjoy the games, parachutes are a great investment. A good, full-sized parachute costs less than $200. With proper care, a parachute that is used regularly should last for several years. To complement your parachute you might want to get some low-cost items such as foam rubber balls, Frisbees, ropes, and a large beach ball.

Summary

While there's no doubt that parachute games are fun, there's also a multitude of benefits that can be gained from this form of play. We can actually practice cooperation, have fun, and end up with everybody feeling like a winner regardless of age, size, or ability. Through imagination we can assume many different roles and with the parachute travel to exciting places. And the leader can join in the fun, too. In short, we think that a parachute is the most exciting, useful, imaginative, and versatile piece of play equipment for groups that we've ever come across.

Leading
Parachute
Games

It's not enough to just throw out a parachute and a couple of foam rubber balls and expect that people will begin playing all these parachute games on their own. It's true that most players will discover the game of Popcorn but just about all the other games require some explanation and leadership. This chapter discusses how to plan and lead a parachute play session.

Leading parachute games is different from leading more traditional and well-known games such as baseball or basketball. First, the rules for parachute games aren't as widely known as the rules of more traditional games. Second, the leader imparts the excitement and joy of the games to the players. This section begins with some ideas on how to be an effective, enthusiastic parachute play leader.

Leading in the Spirit of Play

As the leader your role is to make sure that the game is not only played correctly but is also played well. A game is played correctly when all the rules are followed. A game is played well when the game is being played safely and all the participants are having fun.

Making sure that the group plays the game correctly sometimes requires the leader to be a referee, especially when scores are important. (This is not the case in parachute play.) Having an agreed upon impartial authority frees the players to concentrate on their role in the game without worrying about how everyone else is behaving.

We sometimes do keep score with parachute games (such as in World Record Merry-Go-Round) but only if it enhances play. Rather than concentrating on who won, our main role as leader is to ensure that everyone has an enjoyable time. This shifts our focus to whether the game is being played well, that is, ensuring that everyone has fun and that the play environment is safe. The best way to know if a game is both fun and safe is to be a fellow player in the game. Playing along in the game gives a much different perspective than refereeing the game. If you are having fun as you play the game, it is likely that the other players will also be having fun. If you are bored it is likely the others will also be bored.

As long as everyone is enjoying the game and having a good time, then by all means keep on playing. When the interest in a game begins to wane, change to a different game or put the parachute away for another time. Leave people with a sense of how much fun it is to play with a parachute and they will look forward to the next opportunity to play with it. As with most games, if you play too long people's enthusiasm is likely to fade, and they may not look forward to another parachute play session.

Planning the Play Session

Before the play session begins, give some thought to how much time you have for the session, who will be playing, and where you will be playing. All these factors will help you choose appropriate games. As you play and become more familiar with parachute games, you will develop a sense of how long a game stays fun and which games are appropriate for which settings.

A play session with a parachute can last from 5 to 50 minutes. We don't recommend planning a 50-minute play session the first time you bring out a parachute, though. Give both yourself and your players a chance to get used to the subtlety and nuances of parachute play before you attempt such a long session.

Selecting the Playing Field

Most people would agree that the best place to play with a parachute is outside on a nice day on a level, grassy field. However, we don't always have these ideal conditions, or even a choice of venue. Fortunately you can play with a parachute indoors as well as outdoors. Just make sure you have enough room. Also, don't forget the height when choosing your play space. Balls launched from a parachute can soar pretty high.

Your play field will help you decide which games to play. For example, it is best to play Spin Out on a nice, freshly waxed, slippery, wooden gym floor. This same slippery condition might make it dangerous to play a running game such as Heartbeat. We include recommendations as to the best type of playing field for the games in the descriptions when special considerations need to be made.

Make a List of Games

The single best piece of advice we give all play leaders is to write down a list of games and keep it handy whenever you lead a play session. This gives you something to fall back on if you draw a blank while trying to think of the next game. As you read through this book and become familiar with the games make a list of the ones you think will work best for your situation.

Having a list is so important to us that we had T-shirts printed with a giant games list for the New Games workshops we conducted for community play-festival leaders. We made a mistake by printing the list right side up which meant the text appeared upside down to the wearer. More than once during a festival, excited play leaders would ask strangers to read their shirts to them.

It is very reassuring to have that list of games so close at hand. When you get swept up in the spirit of play and forget everything you planned, you will be able to reach in your pocket, pull out your list, and choose the next game. We usually lead play sessions that include both parachute and nonparachute games, so our games lists include more than just the games in this book. We categorize the games in several ways that are important to us. We divide the games according to activity level (high, medium, or low), number of players, or timing (good beginning, middle, or end games). These categories help you identify the most appropriate games for almost any situation.

Making sure your list includes only the good games that you and your fellow players know and enjoy will ensure that you lead fun play sessions. In other words, this should be a personal list just for you. Please don't just copy down a list of games from a book, not even this book.

You may want to write down a list of games in the order that you want to play them for a specific session. This will certainly add to your confidence as the play leader. Don't be afraid, however, to veer from this predetermined order of games if a better idea appears during the actual play session. Remember, a large element of play is being spontaneous.

During the Play Session

Executing a play session with a parachute is easy. You only need to plan three things: how to begin, how to end, and what to do in the middle.

Getting Started

Starting a play session with a parachute is easy. Roll out the parachute and have everyone grab an edge. Make sure that the players roll the edge in a few times and tuck their fingers under the roll for a good grip. This will also protect the perimeter of the parachute.

Locating and Fetching Equipment and Introducing Ideas

One important job of a play leader is to provide the needed equipment at the right time, so sometimes your role is that of gofer. The game of Popcorn requires foam balls and you are the one to "go fer" them. Have extra sponge balls, Frisbees, and ropes nearby in a duffel bag out of the way until you need them. It's also very easy to delegate this job to other players if you like. We have found that designating reluctant or disruptive players as gofers usually helps bring them into the game.

A play leader is also often a gofer for the rules. Because you are the one who knows how to play the game, you are the leader.

Selecting Teams

Need to split up into two teams? How about players born in the first six months of the year versus players born in the last six months of the year? Or everyone born on an even day of the month against all those born on odd days? You can group astrological signs together into teams, or against one another. Or say, "All those wearing the color blue over there, everyone else over here." We sometimes ask players to instantly raise one hand high with either one or two fingers extended. Keeping their hands up they must find all their teammates who are showing the same number of fingers. If one or two people should change their fingers because they want to be on the same team with a friend, that usually works out okay.

Choosing Volunteers for Special Roles

Kids have a hard time when it comes to picking volunteers. They don't have a well-developed sense of how to wait. If they are not chosen right away, they become frustrated. Instead of asking for volunteers, we try to be more creative.

For instance, we hold spontaneous lotteries to pick our volunteers. We might announce that anyone who is wearing polka dots goes into the middle for Sculpture. After the first round the art pieces get to pick their replacements; as long as it is someone who has not already had a turn. Be careful calling out "blue jeans" to choose someone. That's a great way to pick over half of your group as volunteers. By the way, kids notice if you aren't being fair so watch out about playing favorites.

Just as it is possible to divide into teams by birthdays you can choose volunteers this way. Anyone born in the month of May goes into the middle for the next round. You can group months together if you like or even choose people by seasons if it is appropriate. Sometimes kids will claim they have multiple birthdays so they can get into the middle several times but this usually isn't a major problem.

You can also stand in the middle, close your eyes and spin around with your arm extended. When you stop simply open your eyes, see where your arm is pointing, and choose the nearest person with a raised arm.

Unlike kids, adults are usually reluctant to volunteer. As we get older most of us are increasingly unwilling to take risks or look foolish, especially in front of others. If you, as play leader, are willing to be a volunteer it shows others that there is no reason to be afraid. For the next game the adult players will be more willing to volunteer.

Keeping Things Fun

Along with all the other responsibilities, a frequent role of the leader is that of *enthusiator*, someone who knows the rules and gets the game going in such a way that people want to join in, expecting a fun time. Enthusiasm is contagious. If you enjoy what you are doing and let it show, people will want to try it also.

Hold a Practice Round

Having a hard time trying to persuade people to try out a new game? In order to get people to start playing before they fully understand the rules, we allow them to play a practice round. Because practice doesn't really count, people are willing to try the game even though they may not really understand it. A practice round frequently stops players from asking irrelevant questions before the game begins. During a practice round of Interlocking Gears people can see for themselves where the gears mesh. You won't have to explain it several times.

There is something about not wanting to lose that makes most people wary about trying something they don't fully understand. But you can't lose a practice round; it's only practice. Actually you can't lose any parachute games. We don't have losers; we have players. We don't keep score and give out trophies at the end of the session. Take away the external rewards of scores and prizes and it doesn't matter if people are just practicing or are really playing. Sometimes at the beginning it helps people to think they are only practicing.

The important thing is to have fun. We have found that people have more fun doing things rather than listening to instructions on how to do things. We try to get the games going as quickly as possible, even if it means there is sometimes a little bit of confusion at the start. Calling it practice lets people feel okay about going through the motions even if they don't understand everything. If it is a good game, people will figure it out soon enough.

Discipline When Necessary

If some of your players are acting up then it is your job to make sure they do not disrupt the game. In this case your role may be an authority figure. As the teacher or activity leader, part of your job is to keep the focus. There may be no one perfect way of responding to disruptive behavior. Kids often feel a need to "test" you to see what you will do in a given situation. Responding fairly and even-handedly is best.

One approach we use is to ask disruptive players to sit out for a game. We tell them they are welcome to return to the next game if they can keep from disrupting it. We have found it is important not to explain this in anger. With anger, we only get more resistance. If you do need to ask more than one person to sit out, it's best to have each of them sitting separately. What we are doing is so much fun that people want to play rather than sit out. Putting the responsibility for participation on the players is a tactic that usually works.

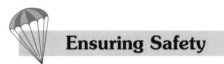 **Ensuring Safety**

Since safety is such an overriding concern, this section covers a wide range of safety issues.

Physical Safety

Most parachute games are inherently safe. Everyone standing in a circle looking at one another creates an awareness of the group that reinforces people's concern for each other's safety. Also, few games involve aggressive contact. However, as leader it is always your responsibility to see that no one gets hurt. It's up to you to keep the game from getting out of control. Being a participant in the game gives you a sense of when the game is starting to become too wild and unsafe.

If you feel that the game is unsafe, stop it or change to a milder version of the same game. A milder version of Cat and Mouse, for example, places the cats down on all fours instead of running around on top of the parachute on just two legs. One of the great things about parachute games is that everyone wants to play them over and over again. This is not true if someone gets injured. An injured player will have to recuperate before she or he can play again, and the entire group tends to get dispirited after an accident.

Again, parachute games are safe. We dislike injuries so much that we are taking time here to help you avoid silly accidents. In the description of the games we point out the few minor safety problems. We also mention some special safety concerns below.

In the game of Spin Out there is a small potential risk of someone getting the parachute wrapped around his or her neck. We just tell the people in the middle to raise their arms in front of them and that the others should stop winding the parachute before it gets to neck level.

When playing Racing Heartbeat some people may want to bring the parachute down too quickly on their fellow players. Just point out that there is a steady rhythm to the game and the object is not to decapitate each other. We also remind people who are changing positions to watch out for others as they run across to avoid collisions.

Notice that we don't even suggest using a parachute to toss people up into the air. Not that this isn't a fun activity, but we can't personally inspect everyone's parachute for strength. Keep in mind that parachutes wear out. A parachute that was great for tossing people last summer may have become too fragile for that purpose this year. Such an activity also puts a great strain on the stitch work, causing the parachute to come apart at the seams or even tear.

We discussed whether we should have a special section explaining how to toss folks safely or not. Then we thought about liability insurance. Then we thought about someone being confined to a wheelchair as a result of one quick, cheap thrill on a parachute. Rather than risk a potential injury by having someone accidentally fall through a parachute, we would just as soon not use a parachute for tossing people.

Emotional Safety

A leader needs to be sensitive to the players' emotional safety when playing with a parachute or when playing other games. Many people have never played with a parachute before and will feel a little bit uncertain about the social appropriateness. Your job as play leader is to invite them into the game and let them feel welcome. You can involve bystanders by just pointing out a gap somewhere on the edge of the parachute and saying, "We could use a few more people over here." On the one hand, don't insist that people play; they should always have the option to sit out. On the other hand, do invite them and make them feel comfortable about joining. Many people need to be sure they are welcome so you might have to extend several invitations. Playful coaxing is a fun, rewarding activity in itself.

Once people are in the game make sure that they don't feel they are being singled out or picked on. We try not to ask for just one volunteer at a time. That way no one feels completely isolated and put in the spotlight. You might want to keep this in mind, though parachute games rarely use solo volunteers. In Spin Out we ask for at least three people at a time. The only game in this book where we ask someone to do something alone is Cat and Mouse. Even then at least two players, the cat and the mouse, participate at the same time. We have found that the spirit of play is enhanced when people get to do things together. Most folks get nervous when we ask them to step outside the group and do something risky such as try to guess what everybody else is thinking. They feel better if they have at least one partner to help them guess.

To summarize our feelings about safety: Parachute games are so much fun we want people to be able to play them over and over again. If they suffer a physical injury, they won't be able to play anymore. If they get too embarrassed, they won't want to play anymore. The group will also be less inclined to participate if they see these things happening to their fellow players.

Summary

The leader knows the rules and creates the mood. The responsibility for making sure things go smoothly, that transitions from one game to the next are timely and appropriate for the feeling of the group, rests on the leader. Other responsibilities include letting everyone feel welcome and safe. Best of all, after explaining the game, the leader becomes a player and leads only when necessary. This last quality is how the parachute play leader differs from a person performing the same role in traditional sports and recreational games. In the next chapter, we look at the skills that are an inherent part of the games.

3

Enhancing Developmental Skills

A child's development consists of acquiring certain social, personal, motor, and perceptual skills during his or her daily activities. As children get older they generally grow bigger, stronger, more agile, and more coordinated. Not everyone acquires these skills at the same rate or to the same degree. Sometimes it becomes painfully obvious that a child has not mastered a skill that for most is simple. A severe manifestation becomes apparent when 5-year-old Jimmy cannot run without stumbling or is not able to walk properly.

Individual differences account for a number of variances in the rate of development. There are three primary factors:

- Children develop coordination at different rates.
- Neurological problems account for some variances.
- Lack of opportunity to practice skills explains other differences.

Parachute games can be useful for this third situation, providing an occasion to improve skills in a way that is fun and exciting.

The games presented in this book aren't intended primarily for developing better skills. The focus is on playing and having fun. People don't play to develop better skills. However, the games do help players improve their

- social skills,
- personal behavior,
- perceptual and physical skills, and
- basic motor skills.

 ## Social Skills

Parachute games expose people to several social skills, including cooperation, trust, problem solving, communication, physical touching, and adaptability. Through the years we have actually seen people grow in and develop their social skills. In this section we will look at specific social skills and suggest games that use and develop these skills. You can then go to the Games Finder on pages 44 to 46 in Part II to locate descriptions of the games.

Cooperation

The following games feature the skill of working together for a common goal.

- Alligator
- Ball Surfing
- Basketball
- Big Bang
- Blow Up
- Cat and Mouse
- Circular Sit-Ups
- Climb the Mountain
- Cop and Robber
- Floating Mushroom
- Flying Parachute
- Free Play
- Ghost Rider
- Group Balance
- Heartbeat
- Housekeeping
- Igloo
- Interlocking Gears
- Jumbo Mushroom
- Lift Off
- Missile Launch
- Mushroom
- Ostrich
- Parachute Golf
- Parachute Volleyball
- Popovers
- Rabbit and Hound
- Racing Heartbeat
- Rocking Chair
- Sculpture
- Shark
- Spin Out
- Swooping Cloud
- Turnover
- Wave Wall
- Who's Peeking?

These games include cooperation as a part of their activity.

- Centipede
- Circular Tug
- Dodge 'em
- I Dare Ya
- It's in the Bag
- Jell-O
- Jellyfish Jaunt
- Machine Wave
- Merry-Go-Round
- Over Under
- Pony Express
- Treasure Hunt
- Waves Overhead
- World Record Merry-Go-Round

Trust

The following games involve building a feeling of group safety.

- Cop and Robber
- Group Balance
- Lift Off
- Racing Heartbeat
- Sculpture
- Wave Rolling

Problem Solving

The games below have as a major characteristic finding one out of many possible solutions.

- Free Play
- Sculpture

These games have problem solving as one feature.

- Cop and Robber
- Cover Up
- Dodge 'em
- Housekeeping
- I Dare Ya
- Parachute Volleyball
- Rabbit and Hound
- Treasure Hunt
- Turnover
- Wave Rolling

Verbal Contact

Games that use interaction with speech (including listening skills) as a major part are as follows.

- Ghost Rider
- Group Balance
- Turnover
- Over Under

These are games where speaking and listening are a part of the game.

- Alligator
- Ball Surfing
- Cat and Mouse
- Circular Tug
- Climb the Mountain
- Cop and Robber
- Dodge 'em
- Floating Mushroom
- Flying Parachute
- Housekeeping
- Igloo
- Interlocking Gears
- I Dare Ya
- Jell-O
- Jellyfish Jaunt
- Jumbo Mushroom
- Lift Off
- Merry-Go-Round
- Mushroom
- Parachute Golf
- Parachute Volleyball
- Pony Express
- Popovers
- Rabbit and Hound
- Raceway
- Racing Heartbeat
- Sculpture
- Shark
- Swooping Cloud
- Treasure Hunt
- Wave Wall
- Who's Peeking
- World Record Merry-Go-Round

Tactile Contact

All of the games include physical contact with the parachute. These particular games require touching other people.

- Alligator
- Cat and Mouse
- Free Play
- Pony Express

- Sculpture
- Shark
- Spin Out
- Turnover

Touching other people is one feature of these games.

- Climb the Mountain
- Cop and Robber
- Gophers
- I Dare Ya
- Jell-O

- Parachute Pass
- Racing Heartbeat
- Top of the Pops
- Waves Overhead
- Wave Rolling

Adaptability

In this context adaptability means how a person's responses fit the actions and movements of others. Following are games that require a high degree of adaptability.

- Cop and Robber
- Dodge 'em
- Gophers
- Heartbeat
- Housekeeping
- Igloo

- Jumbo Mushroom
- Mushroom
- Racing Heartbeat
- Rocking Chair
- Turnover
- Wave Rolling

Adaptability is one property of the following games.

- Alligator
- Ball Surfing
- Centipede
- Circular Sit-Ups
- Circular Tug
- Floating Mushroom
- Flying Parachute

- Free Play
- Ghost Rider
- Group Balance
- I Dare Ya
- Jellyfish Jaunt
- Merry-Go-Round
- Over Under

- Parachute Golf
- Parachute Pass
- Parachute Volleyball
- Popovers
- Rabbit and Hound
- Raceway

- Sculpture
- Shark
- Snake Tag
- Treasure Hunt
- Wave Wall
- World Record Merry-Go-Round

Personal Behavior

The skills of personal behavior considered here are self-control, creativity, spontaneity, and pantomime.

Self-Control

The games below deal with someone's ability to control his or her body, speech, and mind.

- Basketball
- Gophers
- Housekeeping
- I Dare Ya

- Missile Launch
- Sculpture
- Top of the Pops
- Treasure Hunt

Self-control plays a smaller role in these games.

- Alligator
- Ball Surfing
- Big Bang
- Cat and Mouse
- Circular Sit-Ups
- Circular Tug
- Cop and Robber
- Cover Up
- Dodge 'em
- Drag Race
- Floating Mushroom
- Flying Parachute
- Ghost Rider
- Group Balance

- Igloo
- Interlocking Gears
- It's in the Bag
- Jellyfish Jaunt
- Jumbo Mushroom
- Lift Off
- Merry-Go-Round
- Mushroom
- Ostrich
- Over Under
- Parachute Pass
- Parachute Volleyball
- Pony Express
- Popcorn

- Popovers
- Rabbit and Hound
- Raceway
- Racing Heartbeat
- Rocking Chair
- Shark
- Snake Tag
- Wave Machine
- Wave Rolling
- Waves Overhead
- Wave Wall
- Who's Peeking?
- World Record Merry-Go-Round

Creativity

These games require the players to use ideas inventively.

- Free Play
- Sculpture

Creativity is a minor feature of the following games.

- Cover Up
- I Dare Ya
- It's in the Bag
- Jell-O
- Parachute Ride
- Racing Heartbeat
- Turnover
- Wave Rolling

Spontaneity

A notable element of the games below is impromptu actions in the absence of specific directions.

- Alligator
- Dodge 'em
- Free Play
- Sculpture
- Shark
- Turnover
- Who's Peeking?

Spontaneity is also a factor in the following games.

- Blow Up
- Cat and Mouse
- Centipede
- Circular Tug
- Cover Up
- Gophers
- Housekeeping
- I Dare Ya
- Jellyfish Jaunt
- Parachute Pass
- Parachute Ride
- Popcorn
- Popovers
- Top of the Pops
- Wave Rolling

Pantomime

In the succeeding games, an important part is expression through acting movements.

- Alligator
- Shark

Some acting movements are required in the following games.

- Cop and Robber
- It's in the Bag
- Dodge 'em
- Jell-O

Perceptual and Physical Skills

The elements making up perceptual and physical skills are visual ability, skillfulness and coordination, reaction, strength, and endurance.

Visual Ability

These games call for observation and peripheral perception.

- Ball Surfing
- Basketball
- Cat and Mouse
- Cop And Robber
- Dodge 'em
- Gophers
- Housekeeping
- Jell-O
- Missile Launch
- Over Under
- Rabbit and Hound
- Racing Heartbeat
- Top of the Pops
- Treasure Hunt
- Who's Peeking?

Although not an absolute necessity, visual ability is helpful for the following games.

- Centipede
- Circular Tug
- Climb the Mountain
- Floating Mushroom
- Flying Parachute
- Free Play
- Ghost Rider
- Group Balance
- Heartbeat
- I Dare Ya
- Igloo
- Interlocking Gears
- It's in the Bag
- Jellyfish Jaunt

- Jumbo Mushroom
- Lift Off
- Mushroom
- Parachute Golf
- Parachute Pass
- Parachute Ride
- Parachute Volleyball
- Pony Express
- Popcorn

- Popovers
- Raceway
- Sculpture
- Shark
- Snake Tag
- Swooping Cloud
- Wave Rolling
- Wave Wall

Skillfulness and Coordination

These games require complex body movements.

- Ghost Rider
- Gophers
- Igloo

- It's in the Bag
- Pony Express
- Treasure Hunt

These games also have complex body movements, but to a lesser degree.

- Basketball
- Dodge 'em
- Drag Race
- I Dare Ya
- It's in the Bag
- Jell-O
- Merry-Go-Round

- Missile Launch
- Ostrich
- Parachute Pass
- Rocking Chair
- Top of the Pops
- Who's Peeking?
- World Record Merry-Go-Round

Reaction

The games here call for a quick physical response.

- Ball Surfing
- Cat and Mouse
- Climb the Mountain
- Cop and Robber
- Drag Race
- Floating Mushroom
- Flying Parachute

- Gophers
- I Dare Ya
- Parachute Pass
- Popovers
- Top of the Pops
- Treasure Hunt
- Who's Peeking?

These games also need quick reactions, but to a lesser extent.

- Basketball
- Big Bang
- Ghost Rider
- Missile Launch
- Pony Express
- Over Under
- Popcorn
- Rabbit and Hound
- Snake Tag
- Spin Out
- Swooping Cloud
- Wave Wall
- World Record Merry-Go-Round

Strength

The games below require strength in the upper body. They all involve lifting.

- Heartbeat
- Housekeeping
- Lift Off
- Parachute Ride
- Rabbit and Hound
- Racing Heartbeat
- Snake Tag
- Spin Out
- Top of the Pops
- Wave Machine
- Wave Rolling
- Waves Overhead

Strength is one of the elements of the following games.

- Alligator
- Ball Surfing
- Big Bang
- Cat and Mouse
- Circular Sit-Ups
- Circular Tug
- Floating Mushroom
- Flying Parachute
- Ghost Rider
- Jumbo Mushroom
- Mushroom
- Parachute Golf
- Parachute Volleyball
- Popcorn
- Popovers
- Swooping Cloud
- Wave Wall

Endurance

The ability to continue the activity is important here.

- Flying Parachute
- I Dare Ya
- Jellyfish Jaunt
- Popcorn
- Raceway
- Wave Machine
- Wave Rolling
- Waves Overhead

These games require some endurance.

- Cat and Mouse
- Housekeeping
- Merry-Go-Round
- Popovers
- Rabbit and Hound
- Snake Tag
- Top of the Pops
- World Record Merry-Go-Round

Basic Motor Skills

The basic motor skills involved in these games are walking, running, jumping, balancing, leaning, crawling, hopping, and throwing and catching.

Walking

Walking is a major part of these games.

- Interlocking Gears
- Merry-Go-Round

Walking is also a part of these games.

- Centipede
- Jumbo Mushroom
- Over Under
- Parachute Ride
- Shark
- Spin Out

Running

Running is important in the following games.

- Cop and Robber
- Flying Parachute
- Jellyfish Jaunt
- Raceway
- World Record Merry-Go-Round

Running is a part of the following games.

- Basketball
- Housekeeping
- I Dare Ya
- It's in the Bag
- Racing Heartbeat
- Treasure Hunt

Jumping

Jumping is an integral skill for these games.

- Merry-Go-Round
- World Record Merry-Go-Round

Jumping is an element of these games.

- Basketball
- Dodge 'em
- It's in the Bag
- Jell-O
- Missile Launch

Balancing

An ability to keep one's balance is crucial for this game.

- Group Balance

Keeping one's balance is a property of these games as well.

- Circular Tug
- Free Play
- Merry-Go-Round
- Parachute Ride
- Pony Express
- Sculpture
- Spin Out
- Turnover
- World Record Merry-Go-Round

Leaning

These games call for leaning.

- Cat and Mouse
- Pony Express

To a lesser extent, leaning is also used in these games.

- Alligator
- Cop and Robber
- Sculpture

Crawling

These games involve crawling on hands and knees or the stomach.

- Alligator
- Cat and Mouse
- Climb the Mountain
- Dodge 'em
- Free Play
- Gophers
- Jell-O
- Pony Express
- Top of the Pops
- Wave Rolling

Hopping

These games feature hopping on one foot.

- Merry-Go-Round
- World Record Merry-Go-Round

These games can also include hopping.

- I Dare Ya
- Jell-O

Throwing and Catching

These are games in which these skills are a part of the play.

- Basketball
- Dodge 'em
- Gophers
- Housekeeping
- Missile Launch
- Top of the Pops

Throwing and catching can be involved in this game, too.

- Popcorn

4

Caring
for Your
Parachute

So far, so good. You know the benefits of parachute play, how to lead the games, and how games help develop specific skills. If you don't yet have a parachute, don't know where to find one, and/or don't know what to look for when purchasing one you've come to the right chapter. We cover these matters and more.

Purchasing Your Parachute

Not only can you find more places to purchase parachutes these days but also more variety of styles and colors than when we began playing with parachutes. Sports equipment and educational equipment companies are the most common parachute sources. They sell multicolored play parachutes with red, yellow, green, and blue panels. Usually there is mesh over the hole in the middle. Most parachutes come with a storage bag.

If you are lucky, you may still be able to find the big (24 to 30 feet) white cargo parachutes at army-navy surplus stores. Or you might be able to get a parachute from your local skydiving club. Because of the popularity of the new rectangular parachutes, the odds of finding a good round play parachute at a skydiving club are not as great as they used to be. Still, once in a while clubs are willing to part with an antique, round parachute. In any case, a few phone calls are in order.

The cost of the parachute varies with its size and quality, from under $20 for a 6-foot diameter parachute to almost $400 for a 32-foot parachute. Different suppliers charge different prices for the same product.

Size and Strength

Parachutes vary in diameter from 6 to 30 feet (including 12 feet, 20 feet, and 24 feet). A 6-foot parachute is really only good for very young players. Anything much bigger than 30 feet is too bulky and difficult for almost anyone to lift. The material is usually double-stitched, rip-stop nylon that has been chain stitched. This is too bad because if the thread breaks it may unravel. Lock stitching is better. Most companies offer a 1-year warranty against rips and tears acquired during normal usage.

The best way to judge the strength of the material is by its thickness. *Denier* is the term used to measure the thickness of nylon. The higher the denier number, the thicker and, therefore, stronger the material will be. A parachute of 500 denier is stronger than one of 250 denier. Although company representatives may not know what you are talking about right away if you ask what the denier is, it is worthwhile to investigate. We include the denier number (when available) of the parachutes in the following list of parachute outlets.

Getting a Handle on It

Most companies also sell parachutes with handles. Handles make it easier to grab the edge of a parachute, but the number of handles may limit the number of players. It is our experience that even when the handles are sewn on securely, they tend to be the first section of the parachute to deteriorate.

Distributors

Here are some reputable parachute supply companies with which we have had experience. This list is by no means complete. Many suppliers use the same manufacturer so the parachutes are essentially the same. We point out the differences in features and quality that, for the most part, account for the differences in price. Companies are listed alphabetically with their addresses and phone numbers as of this writing. Of course, all this information is subject to change. Contact the suppliers for their most recent prices and product updates.

Front Row Experience
540 Discovery Bay Blvd.
Byron, CA 94514
800-524-9091

Offers parachutes from 12 feet to 30 feet that are made of 200 denier nylon. Flame retardant qualities are unknown. Price range: $53 to $211. The pictures of the game Flying Parachute (page 130) show a Front Row Experience parachute.

Gopher Sport
2929 West Park Drive
Owatonna, MN 55060
800-533-0446

Price range: $19.95 to $199 (see the big parachute pictured in the game Interlocking Gears on page 64).

Palos Sports, Inc.
12235 S. Harlem Ave.
Palos Heights, IL 60463
800-233-5484

Price range: $20 to $155. Hole in the center of the parachutes is open (see the parachute pictured in the game Missile Launch on page 114).

Raven Industries
Rt. 1 Box 123A
County Road 3502
Sulfer Springs, TX 75482
800-298-0728

Price range: $93 to $441. Parachute sizes 12, 19, 22, 26, 28, and 32 feet. Not flame retardant. Parachutes have secure (French fell) seams and are sewn with a lock stitch (very strong). Material is 1.6 ounces per square yard (standard). Parachutes have no handles but have a polypropylene rope sewn in the seam around the circumference. The only company we found that has parachutes in a variety of colors. Middle hole is open. The carrying bag is sold separately.

Snitz Manufacturing
2096 S. Church St.
P.O. Box 76
East Troy, WI 53120
800-558-2224

Three qualities of parachutes: 250 denier single fill, 250 denier double fill, 500 denier double fill. Price range: $18.30 (6 feet) to $186.75 (30 feet). No handles.

Sportime
One Sportime Way
Atlanta, GA 30340-1402
800-444-5700

Price range: $22.50 to $135.50. Size range: 6 to 24 feet.

Toledo P.E. Supply
119 Matzinger
P.O. Box 5618
Toledo, OH 43613
800-225-7749

Price range: $17.99 (6 feet) to $142.99 (30 feet). Parachute is polyester, not nylon. Will repair your parachute after 1 year for a fee.

Repairing Your Parachute

What do you do when you tear your out-of-warranty, more than 1-year-old parachute? Sewing a torn parachute is a good idea, although sewing one by hand is time-consuming. Toledo P.E. Supply is the only company we know that offers a repair service after the warranty expires.

An alternative to sewing is to tape rips with duct tape. Duct tape holds fairly well, but needs replacing every so often. If you have a lot of rips and use a lot of duct tape, your parachute becomes heavy. Parachute repair tape is much lighter and appears to be as strong as duct tape. A bonus is that it is available in the same colors as your parachute. Snitz Manufacturing sells parachute repair tape.

Cleaning Your Parachute

As for washing or cleaning your parachute, the companies' instructions vary considerably. One says to use a washing machine; a second agrees but recommends using a delicate cycle with cold water. Yet another says to dry clean the parachute. The last company representative we asked said not to clean a parachute at all. (He also said never to play on grass!)

Our experience is that it is possible and sometimes necessary to clean parachutes, especially if you play with them outside. Use cold water and make sure the washer is large enough for the size of the parachute. A large parachute requires an industrial-size washing machine. Hot water may shrink the stitching thread and cause the nylon to wrinkle (and generally look weird). Do not put the parachute in the dryer for the same reason. A hot dryer can actually melt the nylon.

Parachutes dry quickly if hung outside or spread out on the grass on a mild day.

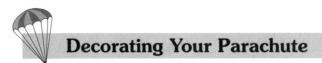

Decorating Your Parachute

If you intend to play games with your parachute then you probably do not want to decorate it. Paint adds weight and peels off during play. However, you might like to spray paint or silk screen words onto your parachute.

You have more decorating options if you plan to use your parachute primarily as a decoration. Fabric and acrylic paints work well with parachutes. You can purchase them at craft or art supply stores. Acrylic inks tend to bleed, which may create a great effect.

Storing and Caring for Your Parachute

Store your parachute in a storage bag in a dry, warm spot. Cool, moist conditions cause mold. Keeping it in its storage bag helps keep moisture out and prevents bits of the parachute from sneaking into trouble, like that spot of grease or oil on the garage floor.

Do not roll up your parachute and use it as a tug-of-war rope. Okay, we know you're thinking, "But what about Circular Tug?" This game puts an even stress on the parachute and therefore is not so harmful.

Summary

Now you're almost ready! You know how to get a parachute; what to look for; and how to repair, clean, decorate, and store it. But you still don't know what to do with it. Not to worry. We devote the rest of the book to games you can play with your parachute.

PART

Learning
the Games

Chapters 5 through 7 are the heart of this book. In them we present 60 great parachute games. Chapter 5 includes the low activity games, chapter 6 the moderate activity games, and chapter 7 the high activity games. You will note that some of the games, though they appear in only one chapter, are classified in two categories, such as low/ moderate, or moderate/high. That's because these borderline games can move from one level of intensity to another depending on how much energy you and your fellow players want to exert.

We present all the games in a format that enables you to understand quickly the requirements and possibilities of each game as you select what to play. After the game description, the following categories may appear:

Safety Considerations appears as a heading when there are important things to consider to make the game safe for all to play.

Activity Level as a category appears only when the activity level of the game is mixed (i.e., low/moderate or moderate/high). Otherwise, the activity level of the game can be determined by the chapter in which it is included or from the Games Finder.

Lead-Ins are games that work well when played before this game.

Number of Players is not often included as a category. That's because "the more the merrier" is almost always true. When it isn't, this heading appears, and we specify what you need to know. Otherwise, just remember that, though a good rule of thumb is to have one player for each panel of the parachute, fewer players can easily spread out around the parachute, and a couple of extra players can always squeeze in. Things start to get crowded when 40 players squeeze around a 24-foot parachute.

Developmental Skills (social, personal behavior, perceptual, and basic motor) are all fundamental to parachute games. We list these skills as primary or secondary, depending on their importance in a particular game. See chapter 3 for more detailed information about developmental skills.

No special motor skills are needed prior to any game; in fact, the games help develop some motor skills.

Additional Equipment is needed to play some of the games. Extra items such as balls or Frisbees are noted here.

Duration of Game is as long as people are having fun. As a general guideline, most games last about 5 minutes. This category appears only when there are special considerations to be made for the length of the game. Remember that arms get tired when playing a game such as Popcorn for longer than a few minutes. On the other hand, certain games such as Spin Out or Cat and Mouse have rounds where only a few players have special (i.e., active) roles. In these cases we recommend having enough time so everyone gets a chance to play one of these roles.

Appropriate Ages for the majority of games are all ages. We note the few exceptions.

When to Play is a tip on the best placement for a game in the context of a play session: beginning, middle, or ending activity.

Where to Play describes the optimal game space. You can play most parachute games almost anywhere. Of course high ceilings are important when playing indoors. A few games require certain playing conditions, in which case this category appears with any special considerations. For example, Spin Out works best on a smooth, hardwood floor.

Follow-Ups include the games that work well after playing this game.

Games Finder

You want to play some parachute games, but with 60 games to choose from, you may feel overwhelmed. We appreciate that fact and provide a Games Finder that will help you make your choices (see pages 44 to 46). The secret is knowing what criteria are important for your particular play situation. Across the top row we have listed the criteria that we think are important, such as activity level (H = high, M = medium, L = low) or when to play (B = beginning game, M = middle game, E = ending game). The names of the games are in the first column of the finder. Scan across the top row to find the criteria that are important to you and then look down the Games Finder to find the characteristics you want. Look in the first column for the name of that game.

Title	p. #	Activity Level	# of Players	Equipment	Appropriate Ages	When to Play
Alligator	90	M				M
Ball Surfing	92	M		large ball	6 or over	M
Basketball	94	M		foam balls	6 or over	M
Big Bang	50	L		foam balls	6 or over	M
Blow Up	52	L				M
Cat and Mouse	128	H				M
Centipede	95	L/M				M
Circular Sit-Ups	96	M				M
Circular Tug	98	M	24 or fewer	marker		M
Climb the Mountain	100	M			6-60	E
Cop and Robber	102	M				M
Cover Up	53	L				M
Dodge 'em	104	M		foam balls		M
Drag Race	54	L				E
Floating Mushroom	56	L			6 or over	M
Flying Parachute	130	H	24 or fewer			M
Free Play	58	L		foam balls, frames		B
Ghost Rider	105	M			6 or over	M
Gophers	106	M		foam balls		M
Group Balance	60	L				E

Activity	Page	Level	Players	Equipment	Group	Code
Heartbeat	108	M				B
Housekeeping	132	H		foam balls		M
I Dare Ya	134	H				M
Igloo	62	L				M
Interlocking Gears	64	L	12 or more	second parachute		M
It's in the Bag	110	M	fewer than 24	storage bag		E
Jell-O	136	H				M
Jellyfish Jaunt	137	H	12 or more			M
Jumbo Mushroom	66	L				B
Lift Off	112	M	12 or more		12 or over	M
Merry-Go-Round	138	H				M
Missile Launch	114	M		foam balls	6 or over	M
Mushroom	68	L				B
Ostrich	70	L				M
Over Under	72	L			6 or over	M
Parachute Golf	74	L		ball		M
Parachute Pass	76	L				E
Parachute Ride	77	L	fewer than 12			E
Parachute Volleyball	116	M	12 or more	2nd parachute, ball	6 or over	M
Pony Express	141	H				M
Popcorn	144	M/H		foam balls		B

(continued)

(continued)

Title	p. #	Activity Level	# of Players	Equipment	Appropriate Ages	When to Play
Popovers	118	M		foam balls		M
Rabbit and Hound	78	L		2 balls		M
Raceway	146	H				M
Racing Heartbeat	147	H				M
Rocking Chair	79	L				M
Sculpture	80	L				M
Shark	120	M		Frisbee(s)		M
Snake Tag	150	M/H		ropes		M
Spin Out	122	L/M				M
Swooping Cloud	82	L			6 or over	M
Top of the Pops	152	H		foam balls		M
Treasure Hunt	124	M		assorted objects		M
Turnover	84	L				E
Wave Machine	125	M				B
Wave Rolling	154	M/H				M
Waves Overhead	126	M				M
Wave Wall	86	L				M
Who's Peeking?	87	L				M
World Record Merry-Go-Round	156	H		marker		M

We suggest that you photocopy this finder so you'll have it handy when you lead games. If you have other criteria that aren't listed here, you may want to design your own games finder.

As you lead and play the games and become more familiar with them, you may choose to eliminate the finder and just keep a list of games in your pocket. If you get stuck for a game in the middle of a game session you can just pull out your list for a quick idea. That's what we do.

Here are three sample play sessions that have worked well for us. You might want to start out with these groupings, but the longer you play, the more you'll develop your own way of doing things and your own favorite game combinations. Don't be limited by our experience. Go out there and play, express yourself, and have a good time!

Sample Play Sessions

1. Wave Machine
2. Mushroom
3. Jumbo Mushroom
4. Igloo
5. Rocking Chair
6. Heartbeat
7. Racing Heartbeat
8. Cat and Mouse
9. Climb the Mountain
10. Drag Race

1. Free Play
2. Merry-Go-Round
3. World Record Merry-Go-Round
4. Snake Tag
5. Shark
6. Centipede
7. Spin Out
8. Circular Tug
9. Group Balance
10. Turnover

1. Popcorn
2. Big Bang
3. Gophers
4. Circular Sit-Ups
5. Ostrich
6. Blow Up
7. Cop and Robber
8. Ghost Rider
9. Turnover
10. It's in the Bag

Low Activity Parachute Games

Here are 23 games that give you a chance to rest and play at the same time. Even people who have limited mobility can play these games; or they can be used with any group when you want to keep things low key, or to take a breather after you've worn yourselves out with high activity games.

Big Bang

Big Bang

Have everyone spread the parachute on the ground and then place all the balls in the middle. "One, two, three, lift!" The players lift the parachute as quickly as possible to shoulder level and then snap it down. The effect is to have the balls fly off the parachute. Congratulations, you have just demonstrated the big bang theory of how the universe began with one giant explosion.

For a little variety, try this with one large ball.

Lead-Ins: Popcorn, Floating Mushroom, Heartbeat, Igloo, other mushroom games.

Developmental Skills: Primary—cooperation; Secondary—self-control, reaction, strength.

Additional Equipment: Foam balls or other light, soft objects.

Duration of Game: Repeating this game numerous times takes about 3 minutes.

Appropriate Ages: Players under age 6 might have trouble lifting a large parachute.

When to Play: Middle.

Where to Play: Indoor space needs a high ceiling with protected lights.

Follow-Ups: Ghost Rider, Ball Surfing, Popcorn, Housekeeping, Popovers, Parachute Golf.

Blow Up

Blow Up can be considered a continuation of Ostrich in which the object of the game is to try to keep the parachute inflated. It takes a concerted effort with all the players using just their lungs and breath to keep the parachute up as long as possible. Don't be disheartened; the parachute settles to the ground eventually. By the way, this is great practice for blowing out birthday candles.

Lead-Ins: Ostrich, Who's Peeking?

Developmental Skills: Primary—cooperation; Secondary—spontaneity.

Duration of Game: A miracle if this lasts more than a minute.

When to Play: Middle.

Follow-Ups: Any game, especially moderate or high activity ones.

Cover Up

Have everyone lie down on their own section of a loosely laid out parachute. The game is to see if everyone can find enough spare fabric at the same time to tuck themselves in. You can vary the activity by calling out specific body parts to wrap.

Lead-Ins: Centipede, Raceway, Flying Parachute, Treasure Hunt, Spin Out, Shark.

Developmental Skills: Secondary—problem solving, creativity, spontaneity, self-control.

Duration of Game: Only a few minutes.

When to Play: Middle.

Follow-Ups: Sculpture, Jellyfish Jaunt, Dodge 'em, Top of the Pops, Rocking Chair.

Drag Race

Drag Race

When you are finished playing with the parachute don't just tell people you are through and get stuck packing it up alone. Instead, trick the players into helping you roll up the parachute.

Our game is called Drag Race. It's easy to play, it's fun, and it quickly reduces the parachute into a nice, small bundle. Everyone is a drag racer. The object is to be the first drag racer to the middle of the parachute. You get there by rolling up the parachute with your hands. Sound effects help. "Racers start your engines. And they're off. Vroom!"

Safety Considerations: As players get closer to the middle, there is bound to be physical contact. Simply remind them not to damage other "racers."

Lead-Ins: Parachute Ride, Cover Up, I Dare Ya, any moderate or high activity game.

Developmental Skills: Primary—reaction; Secondary—self-control, skillfulness and coordination.

Duration of Game: About 1 minute.

When to Play: A perfect ending game.

Follow-Ups: It's in the Bag, Parachute Ride.

Floating Mushroom

Floating Mushroom

Floating Mushroom starts the same as Mushroom, but this time the players lift the parachute over their heads. When the leader gives a predetermined signal, such as "Now!", or "Let go!", or "Fungus Fly Free!", everyone releases the parachute simultaneously, or at least tries to. (It's fun to caution the players that if everyone lets go of the parachute at exactly the same time, it just might keep on floating all the way up to the sky.)

Safety Considerations: Encourage players to simply watch the parachute until it is all the way down. Children often have the desire to run into the parachute as it descends, which can be a lot of fun—until they run into each other at full speed.

Lead-Ins: Mushroom, Jumbo Mushroom, Big Bang, Climb the Mountain, Heartbeat.

Developmental Skills: Primary—cooperation, reaction; Secondary—verbal contact, adaptability, self-control, visual ability, strength.

Duration of Game: This game can be repeated a few times but is still over in minutes.

Appropriate Ages: Very young children (under 6 years) have trouble letting go together.

When to Play: Middle.

Where to Play: Indoor space should have a high ceiling.

Follow-Ups: Jell-O, Sculpture, Dodge 'em, Centipede, any high activity game.

Free Play

This parachute game may be obvious, but we are mentioning it to cover all bases. Very often people like to play with the parachute without any set game. Just put the parachute out and let the players experiment. It's fun to see what can happen.

Safety Considerations: We recommend that someone continue to watch over the activity, even though he or she is doing so passively. There are a couple of reasons for this. We would not want to see a claustrophobic player trapped in a seemingly hopeless tangle of parachute. Sometimes kids think covering someone else is a great game and don't realize that it looks like more fun from the outside than from the inside.

Tossing someone up can be fun but can also be very dangerous. Actually, the tossing up part is always fun. It's the sudden stop if someone hits the ground that can be dangerous. Remember, army-surplus parachutes are no longer strong enough to stop someone from falling. That's why they are surplus!

Free Play

Specially made play parachutes were never designed to stop people from falling. In addition, no matter how strong the parachute was the last time you used it, chances are that other people have used it since then and it may be a parachute just waiting for a rip. We don't want to scare you, but we also want to make sure that no one gets hurt.

Lead-Ins: Wave Rolling, Gophers, Jell-O, Cover Up, Merry-Go-Round.

Developmental Skills: Primary—cooperation, problem solving, tactile contact, creativity, spontaneity, crawling; Secondary—adaptability, visual ability, balancing.

Additional Equipment: Possibly foam balls or frames to place under the parachute.

When to Play: Beginning.

Follow-Ups: Waves Overhead, I Dare Ya, Cop and Robber, Merry-Go-Round.

Group Balance

Group Balance

Make sure everyone has a good grip on the parachute, and then tell everyone to lean back slowly at the same time. (Remember to roll up the edge several times with your fingers tucked in under the roll before leaning.)

The parachute gets tighter and tighter, but a good strong parachute can support that type of evenly distributed tension. If everyone works together, all the players should be able to lean back quite far without losing their balance. If not, you get to find out which side of the parachute weighs the most! Oof!

For an added challenge, ask participants to turn their backs to the parachute, reach behind themselves for a grip, and then try to balance facing outward.

Safety Considerations: Should be played on a soft surface such as grass or mats, especially if players are worried about falling.

Lead-Ins: Circular Sit-Ups, Spin Out, Merry-Go-Round, Dodge 'em, Shark, Wave Wall.

Developmental Skills: Primary—cooperation, trust, verbal contact, balancing; Secondary—adaptability, self-control, visual ability.

Duration of Game: Likely only to last a few minutes.

When to Play: Ending.

Follow-Ups: Circular Tug, Ball Surfing, Ghost Rider, Lift Off, Drag Race.

Igloo

Igloo

Lift the parachute up into a giant mushroom, take a couple of steps in, and bring the parachute down behind you with everyone inside the parachute sitting on the edge. You have just built the warmest igloo in the world. Not only does it look great from the outside, but from the inside it's a wonderful place for telling secrets or playing the classic game of Telephone. And when it's time to get out, "The last one out is a turnip!"

Lead-Ins: Jumbo Mushroom, Heartbeat, other mushroom games.

Developmental Skills: Primary—cooperation, adaptability, skillfulness and coordination; Secondary—verbal contact, self-control, visual ability.

When to Play: Middle.

Follow-Ups: Rocking Chair, Blow Up, Centipede, Waves Overhead.

Interlocking Gears

Interlocking Gears

This game requires two parachutes. Place the two parachutes side-by-side so they are almost touching. Both groups walk in a circle as in the Merry-Go-Round game. When players reach the point where the two parachutes meet, they grab hold of the other parachute, let go of the one they are holding, and join the other circle. This means that people are walking in a giant figure eight pattern (one circle rotates clockwise; the other counterclockwise). It takes timing and coordination between the two groups but eventually it goes like clockwork. After a while, have players reverse directions.

Lead-Ins: Flying Parachute, Wave Rolling, Parachute Golf, any other high activity game.

Number of Players: 12 or more.

Developmental Skills: Primary—walking, cooperation; Secondary—self-control, visual ability, verbal contact.

Additional Equipment: Second parachute.

When to Play: Middle.

Where to Play: You need enough room to spread out two parachutes.

Follow-Ups: Parachute Volleyball, Sculpture, Merry-Go-Round, Missile Launch.

Jumbo Mushroom

Jumbo Mushroom

Similar to Mushroom, but this time as you lift the parachute ask everyone to walk in a step or two. This makes the mushroom grow even bigger. Repeat the game with everyone taking an additional step. Each round makes the mushroom bigger, and eventually everyone meets in the middle.

Safety Considerations: Have everyone slowly count out loud and step into the center together so there are no high-speed collisions.

Lead-Ins: Mushroom, Heartbeat, Floating Mushroom, any more active game.

Developmental Skills: Primary—cooperation, adaptability; Secondary—verbal contact, self-control, visual ability, strength, walking.

When to Play: Beginning.

Where to Play: Requires a tall ceiling if played indoors.

Follow-Ups: Moderate or high activity game, Floating Mushroom, other mushroom games.

Mushroom

Mushroom

Here is something that involves teamwork, is not too hard, and looks beautiful. Everyone kneels down and holds the parachute taut on the ground. On the same count everyone stands up, lifting the parachute high up over their heads. A giant mushroom is formed. Have the players stand still and watch as the parachute slowly settles back down to the ground.

Having a hard time getting everyone to begin on the same count? One way to get people to lift the parachute together is on the universal word "Mushroom." Calling out preliminary vegetables such as "Broccoli" or "Asparagus" builds up the suspense.

Lead-Ins: Wave Machine, Free Play, popcorn games, any high activity games.

Developmental Skills: Primary—cooperation, adaptability; Secondary—verbal contact, self-control, visual ability, strength.

When to Play: Beginning.

Where to Play: Requires a tall ceiling if played indoors.

Follow-Ups: Jumbo Mushroom, Floating Mushroom, or a moderate or high activity game.

Ostrich

Ostrich

Here's a great game that looks as funny from the inside as it does from the outside. Everyone hoists the parachute and takes two steps in to form a Jumbo Mushroom. While the mushroom is descending get down on your stomach or your knees, poke your head under the parachute and pull the parachute down around your shoulders. The view from the inside is a ring of disembodied smiling faces all looking at each other as the parachute slowly settles to the ground. Don't even think about what you look like to the people on the outside. It's best to pretend you are invisible to everyone but fellow ostriches.

Vary the game by reversing the process: bodies under the parachute and heads sticking out.

Lead-Ins: Circular Tug, Climb the Mountain, any other moderate or high activity game.

Developmental Skills: Primary—cooperation; Secondary—self-control, skillfulness and coordination.

Duration of Game: This game will likely last only a minute or two, at most.

When to Play: Middle.

Where to Play: Not on dirt, concrete, or blacktop.

Follow-Ups: Cat and Mouse, Circular Sit-Ups, Cover Up.

Over Under

Over Under

Want to turn the parachute over quickly? Make a mushroom and have one side let go of the parachute. Then have both sides trade positions as fast as possible. Watch out for the parachute.

Lead-Ins: Turnover, Floating Mushroom, Heartbeat, any mushroom game.

Developmental Skills: Primary—verbal contact, visual ability; Secondary—cooperation, adaptability, walking, self-control, reaction.

Appropriate Ages: 6 and over.

When to Play: Middle.

Follow-Ups: Flying Parachute, Circular Tug, Jell-O, Sculpture.

Parachute Golf

Parachute Golf

If your parachute has a hole in the middle you can play a round of Parachute Golf. It takes quite a bit of teamwork to get the ball to roll through the hole. We would guess about a par 47.

For young children, a smaller ball makes it easier to get a hole-in-one.

Lead-Ins: Ball Surfing, Ghost Rider, Popovers, Wave Machine, Popcorn.

Developmental Skills: Primary—cooperation; Secondary—verbal contact, adaptability, visual ability, strength.

Additional Equipment: A ball small enough to go through the hole in the parachute.

Duration of Game: Length of game may vary from 5 to 15 minutes.

When to Play: Middle.

Follow-Ups: Housekeeping, Missile Launch, Rabbit and Hound, Snake Tag.

Parachute Pass

In this game all the players stand still and pass a bit of the parachute to their neighbor. The parachute is passed from hand to hand but the players are not allowed to cross their arms. One hand should be holding on at all times. The object is for you to try to pass faster than you receive. You are doing a good job if there is a lot of loosely draped parachute by the neighbor you are passing to, while on your other side the parachute is tight.

Lead-Ins: Group Balance, Circular Tug, any mushroom, popcorn, or more active game.

Developmental Skills: Primary—reaction; Secondary—self-control, skillfulness and coordination, tactile contact, adaptability, spontaneity, visual ability.

Duration of Game: 1 to 2 minutes.

When to Play: Ending.

Follow-Ups: Drag Race, It's in the Bag, Group Balance, Circular Sit-Ups.

Parachute Ride

Parachutes don't always have to be round or fully extended in order to have fun with them. It's true that not many people can participate in a parachute ride at any one time, but for the lucky one or two who do get a lift, it's a memorable ride.

Safety Considerations: Make sure that the person(s) pulling the parachute doesn't go over any harmful surfaces, such as rocks or holes.

Lead-Ins: Climb the Mountain, Merry-Go-Round, I Dare Ya, Jell-O.

Number of Players: Fewer than 12.

Developmental Skills: Primary—strength; Secondary—visual ability, walking, balancing, creativity, spontaneity.

When to Play: Ending.

Where to Play: Best on a slippery surface.

Follow-Ups: Free Play, Spin Out, Lift Off, Drag Race, It's in the Bag.

Rabbit and Hound

Throw two unlike balls on top of the parachute. Two teams try to control the destiny of the two balls: One ball is the hound, the other is the rabbit. One team tries to help the hound catch the rabbit while the other team is trying to help the rabbit get away.

The teams can be divided several different ways, and each arrangement results in different team strategies. You can draw an imaginary line down the middle of the parachute to divide the teams, or create teams that consist of every other person around the edge. An interesting variation might be to divide the parachute into quarters and have the two opposing quadrants work together as a team.

Lead-Ins: Ball Surfing, Housekeeping, Basketball, any other ball games.

Developmental Skills: Primary—cooperation, visual ability, strength; Secondary—problem solving, verbal contact, adaptability, self-control, reaction, endurance.

Additional Equipment: Two different types or colors of balls; a basketball and a volleyball work well.

Duration of Game: This game could end quickly, and roles could be reversed and played again for another round. In any case, game ends in 2 to 3 minutes.

When to Play: Middle.

Follow-Ups: Gophers, Missile Launch, Parachute Golf, Parachute Volleyball.

Rocking Chair

While the players are still inside an Igloo, they can make a giant Rocking Chair. Instead of rocking back and forth, this rocking chair tends to rock in a circular motion. Can you make it rock in both a clockwise and then a counterclockwise direction? Begin with small movements. Before too long a group rhythm develops and then gets amplified.

Lead-Ins: Igloo, Centipede, Ostrich, any high activity game.

Developmental Skills: Primary—cooperation, adaptability; Secondary—self-control, skillfulness and coordination.

When to Play: Middle.

Follow-Ups: Moderate or high activity game.

Sculpture

Sculpture

Ask three to six players to go underneath the parachute while everyone else makes a mushroom. The players in the middle form themselves into a living sculpture as the parachute settles down around them. Some go high, some go low, and all together they form a giant piece of modern art. Once the parachute descends we can all admire the wrapped artwork.

Finally, the sculpture is ready, and it's time to unveil the work of art. If you like you can make a guessing game before the unveiling to see if people on the outside of the parachute can guess what the form is or who is making what shape.

Lead-Ins: I Dare Ya, Racing Heartbeat, Gophers, Flying Parachute, Merry-Go-Round.

Developmental Skills: Primary—cooperation, trust, problem solving, tactile contact, creativity, spontaneity, self-control; Secondary—adaptability, balancing, verbal contact, visual ability, leaning.

When to Play: Middle.

Follow-Ups: Jellyfish Jaunt, World Record Merry-Go-Round, Pony Express, Raceway.

Swooping Cloud

Swooping Cloud

This game begins like the Floating Mushroom, but not everyone lets go at the same time. In fact, one side intentionally lets go after the other side. The parachute will then make a swooping cloud as it rises up on one side and comes right back down to the ground on the other side.

Lead-Ins: Floating Mushroom, Mushroom, Heartbeat, any mushroom game.

Developmental Skills: Primary—cooperation; Secondary—verbal contact, visual ability, reaction, strength.

Duration of Game: This is a very short game that can be repeated many times in just a few minutes.

Appropriate Ages: Players under age 6 might have trouble lifting a large parachute.

When to Play: Middle.

Where to Play: Very low ceilings make this game difficult.

Follow-Ups: Over Under, Flying Parachute, any moderate or high activity game.

Turnover

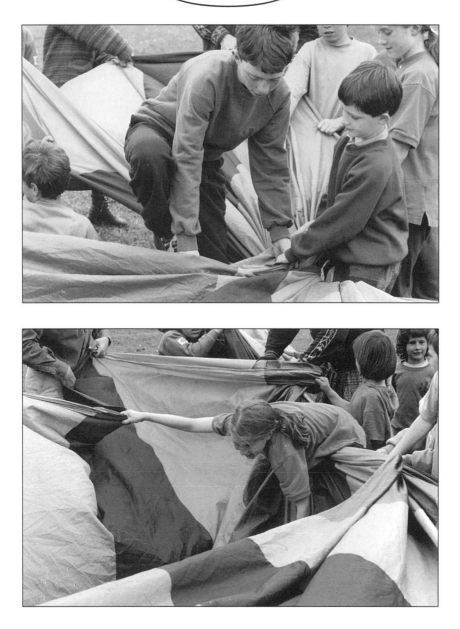

Turnover

Here's a group challenge. Can you turn the parachute over with no one letting go of the edge? It takes lots of teamwork and communication. Oh, and some trust and delicate footwork are helpful, too.

Lead-Ins: Over Under, Jellyfish Jaunt, Parachute Pass, Centipede, Circular Tug.

Developmental Skills: Primary—cooperation, verbal contact, tactile contact, adaptability, spontaneity; Secondary—problem solving, creativity, balancing.

When to Play: Ending.

Follow-Ups: Sculpture, Jell-O, Cop and Robber, Circular Sit-Ups.

Wave Wall

Hold the parachute still and have one small arc of people send a wave across the ocean to the other side. Did it get there? Can the people who received the wave pass on an even bigger one to another arc of the parachute? How big can these tidal waves get? What happens when two waves meet in the center?

Lead-Ins: Swooping Cloud, Parachute Golf, Big Bang, any mushroom game.

Developmental Skills: Primary—cooperation; Secondary—self-control, visual ability, strength, verbal contact, adaptability, reaction.

Duration of Game: This game may last only 2 or 3 minutes.

When to Play: Middle.

Follow-Ups: Over Under, Popovers, Rabbit and Hound, Ghost Rider, Ball Surfing.

Who's Peeking?

While you are playing Ostrich, you can also play this favorite game of ours. We call it Who's Peeking?. The object is to have everyone close their eyes and then see who is peeking. The best players are the ones who can catch the others peeking without getting caught themselves. We saw that, you're peeking!

Lead-Ins: Ostrich, Igloo, Rocking Chair, Raceway.

Developmental Skills: Primary—cooperation, spontaneity, visual ability, reaction; Secondary—verbal contact, self-control, skillfulness and coordination.

Duration of Game: This game won't last longer than 2 to 3 minutes.

When to Play: Middle.

Where to Play: Not on dirt, concrete, or blacktop.

Follow-Ups: Wave Wall, Alligator, Parachute Pass, Over Under, any more active game.

Moderate Activity
Parachute Games

To help you vary the energy level of your play session, we include in this chapter 22 games that we consider moderately active.

Alligator

This is a less active variation of the high-energy game, Shark. Instead of standing, all the players sit with their legs underneath the parachute. The player chosen to be the alligator crawls under the parachute to enter the swamp.

The exciting part of this game is when the alligator gets hungry. What hungry alligator could resist all those delicious legs floating at the edge of the swamp? If you get "bitten," you become the alligator; and the "old" alligator joins the rest of the group. If someone does not want to be eaten by an alligator or has already been an alligator and wants to let others have a chance to chomp, that player should sit with legs crossed underneath himself or herself instead of under the parachute.

Instead of just biting unsuspecting players as in Shark, alligators can actually grab hold of someone's leg and gently drag them under the parachute. Watching a fellow wader go under makes quite an impression on the survivors at the swamp's edge.

In another version the players do not switch roles. Alligators create new alligators by biting waders and remain alligators until the end. The game is over when the swamp is full of alligators and no players are left to munch.

Alligator

Safety Considerations: Alligators who are too rough on waders may need a reminder that this is just for fun.

Lead-Ins: Group Balance, Raceway, Circular Sit-Ups, Ghost Rider, popcorn games.

Developmental Skills: Primary—cooperation, tactile contact, spontaneity, pantomime, crawling; Secondary—strength, leaning, verbal contact, adaptability, self-control.

When to Play: Middle.

Follow-Ups: Cat and Mouse, Cover Up, Missile Launch, Circular Tug, Ball Surfing.

Ball Surfing

Ball Surfing

Place a large ball on top of a flat parachute and roll it around the edge. Players should lift the parachute just after the ball passes by. Timing is critical. If someone lifts up a section of the parachute too soon, the ball slows down and stops. If someone lifts a section too late, the ball either runs into the player or rolls off the parachute.

The smaller the ball the greater the challenge. The larger the ball the easier the game will be and the greater the effect. This game is even more fun with an Earthball.

Lead-Ins: Group Balance, Circular Tug, Dodge 'em, Ghost Rider, popcorn games.

Developmental Skills: Primary—cooperation, visual ability, reaction; Secondary—adaptation, self-control, strength, verbal contact.

Additional Equipment: A large ball.

Appropriate Ages: A challenge for the under 6's.

When to Play: Middle.

Follow-Ups: Wave Wall, Merry-Go-Round, Parachute Volleyball, Cop and Robber.

Basketball

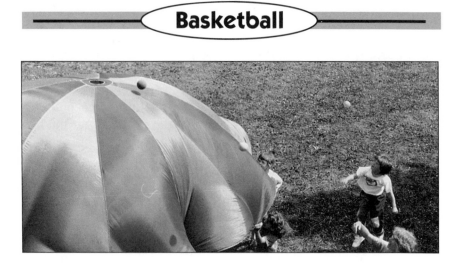

Even Michael Jordan would find it hard to dunk in this game, because the "basket" is the hole in the middle of the parachute, high atop a mushroom.

Four or five players, each with a ball, stand outside the edge of the parachute while the other players raise the parachute into a mushroom. Once the parachute is up, the shooters attempt to score baskets by throwing a ball through the hole. See how many balls get through the hole in one mushroom, or how many mushrooms it takes to get one ball through. Naturally, you want to alternate players to give everyone a chance, after about five mushrooms. This may not get you on the All-Stars; but it is a challenge, and it sure is fun.

Lead-Ins: Missile Launch, Housekeeping, Big Bang, Popcorn, Top of the Pops.

Developmental Skills: Primary—throwing and catching, self-control, visual ability, cooperation; Secondary—skillfulness and coordination, reaction, running, jumping.

Additional Equipment: A foam ball for each basket shooter.

Appropriate Ages: The under 6 age group may find this difficult.

When to Play: Middle.

Follow-Ups: Group Balance, Circular Sit-Ups, Spin Out, Flying Parachute.

Centipede

Have you ever gone on a group hike? Here is a way to guarantee that there aren't any stragglers. All players help to lift the parachute up over their heads; then they all step underneath and let the parachute settle down over them. Once everyone is comfortably covered by the parachute, it is time to begin the walk. Watching the centipede is as much fun as being the centipede; you might want to divide the group into scientists and bugs and give everyone a chance to be on each side.

Safety Considerations: The end result looks like a very obese, undisciplined centipede. For this reason, it is good to appoint someone to be the "brain of the centipede." The brain directs activities and avoids collisions. Curiously enough, this centipede's brain lives outside the parachute. It baffles biologists but makes for a safer game.

Activity Level: Low/moderate.

Lead-Ins: Blow Up, Waves Overhead, Racing Heartbeat, any game.

Developmental Skills: Secondary—cooperation, adaptability, spontaneity, visual ability, walking.

When to Play: Middle.

Where to Play: You will need a good amount of space around the parachute for walking.

Follow-Ups: Jellyfish Jaunt, Flying Parachute, Cop and Robber, most any game.

Circular Sit-Ups

Circular Sit-Ups

We find normal sit-ups a bit boring. We feel it's easier, and certainly more fun, to perform one giant circular sit-up.

Have everyone sit along the edge of the parachute with feet and legs underneath. Hold on tight. One section starts to lean back while the opposite side leans forward. The two sides continue in this manner to create a see-saw effect. The whole group is doing sit-ups, sort of. Those on the sides merely sway from side to side. That was just a warm up for Circular Sit-Ups.

The movement you need for circular sit-ups is similar to the round-about rocking motion of Rocking Chair, rather than the straight up-and-down motion of a traditional sit-up. If every player circles from the waist the parachute will move accordingly. For the group to master this collective movement you as leader may need to orchestrate the players a little. Point out which section of the parachute should be leaning back and then circling to the side until the players get the hang of it. Once the group has mastered both clockwise and counter-clockwise sit-ups, try reversing directions without stopping.

Lead-Ins: Igloo, Merry-Go-Round, World Record Merry-Go-Round, Dodge 'em.

Developmental Skills: Primary—cooperation; Secondary—adaptability, strength, self-control.

Duration of Game: Players probably won't want to play more than a minute or two.

When to Play: Middle.

Follow-Ups: Group Balance, Circular Tug, Ball Surfing, Spin Out, Alligator.

Circular Tug

Circular Tug

This is an inverted version of Group Balance. Instead of everyone working together to stay balanced, the players compete in a circular tug-of-war. Everyone rolls up the edge of the parachute a few times and pulls straight back to see which side (or arc) of the parachute is the strongest. For those who like to see how they are doing, place a ball, Frisbee, or other marker on the ground underneath the middle of the parachute to start. Don't get pulled over the marker!

A challenging variation of this game is to ask participants to turn their backs to the parachute, reach behind themselves for a grip, and then have a tug.

Lead-Ins: Group Balance, Alligator, any mushroom, popcorn, or low activity game.

Number of Players: 24 or fewer.

Developmental Skills: Secondary—cooperation, adaptability, strength, verbal contact, self-control, spontaneity, visual ability, balancing.

Additional Equipment: A Frisbee or a ball as a marker.

Appropriate Ages: All ages can play, but make sure players of different ages and sizes are spread out evenly around the parachute.

When to Play: Middle.

Follow-Ups: Shark, Ball Surfing, Circular Sit-Ups, Merry-Go-Round, Jellyfish Jaunt, Ghost Rider, any mushroom, popcorn, or low activity game.

Climb the Mountain

Climb the Mountain

First make a giant mushroom. Then on a given verbal signal, such as "Down!", bring the parachute down quickly and hold the edge down with your knees. This traps the air underneath the parachute. Now pretend to be a mountain climber and on your knees, try to scramble up the snowy mountain of cloth using just your arms.

Safety Considerations: As enthusiastic climbers reach the middle, you may want to remind them to watch out for fellow climbers' heads on the other side of the mountain. Also, make it clear to players they should not go under the parachute in this game.

Lead-Ins: Mushroom, Big Bang, Floating Mushroom, Wave Wall, Ostrich, any game.

Developmental Skills: Primary—cooperation, reaction, crawling; Secondary—verbal contact, tactile contact, visual ability.

Appropriate Ages: Between 6 and 60; younger and older players might find the game a bit too physical.

When to Play: Ending.

Where to Play: Best played on a soft surface.

Follow-Ups: Drag Race, Circular Sit-Ups, Group Balance, It's in the Bag, any low activity game.

Cop and Robber

Cop and Robber

"Stop! Thief!" And the chase is on. The robber makes a dash for her hideout. Her gang attempts to close ranks after her, thereby keeping the cop out. Actually, the robber can go underneath or outside the parachute while the cop tries to follow. The players around the parachute let the robber in or out but close ranks to prevent the cop from following.

Justice is served when the robber gets caught. Then it's time to choose a new cop and a new robber. Later, try introducing two cops and two robbers.

Safety Considerations: If the robbers around the parachute are too rough on the cop, you may need to ask them to give the long arm of the law a chance. After all, the chase is the fun part.

Lead-Ins: Shark, Flying Parachute, Pony Express, Waves Overhead, Popcorn.

Developmental Skills: Primary—cooperation, trust, adaptability, visual ability, reaction, running; Secondary—problem solving, verbal contact, tactile contact, self-control, pantomime, leaning.

When to Play: Middle.

Follow-Ups: Alligator, Wave Rolling, Jellyfish Jaunt, Merry-Go-Round, Centipede.

Dodge 'em

Here is a nice variation on that classic old game, "dodge ball." We use soft foam balls instead of playground balls because the distance is so much shorter and foam is less dangerous. A few players go under the parachute; everyone else holds the parachute about head high. The added challenge is to have someone try to throw the ball while holding on to the parachute with one hand and bending over. This feat is nicely balanced by the dodger having to deal with an ever-present parachute that restricts every movement.

Lead-Ins: Alligator, Heartbeat, Ostrich, Missile Launch, any low or high activity game.

Developmental Skills: Primary—adaptability, spontaneity, visual ability, crawling, throwing and catching; Secondary— cooperation, problem solving, self-control, verbal contact, pantomime, skillfulness and coordination, jumping.

Additional Equipment: One or two foam balls, perhaps more for younger children.

When to Play: Middle.

Follow-Ups: Treasure Hunt, Waves Overhead, Who's Peeking?, Basketball.

Ghost Rider

A long time ago there lived a daredevil motorcycle rider. He loved to ride his motorcycle faster and faster and jump over taller and taller obstacles. One day he and his motorcycle jumped so high that he rode into a cloud. The moisture in the cloud fouled his carburetor and he crashed to the ground.

The spirit of the Ghost Rider can sometimes be invoked. Everyone holds on to the edge of the parachute with both hands. One player raises his arms and quickly brings them down again. The player next to him on one side follows, and then the next player in line, and so on. This movement creates a giant, circular, rolling wave.

A well-coordinated wave creates a jet of air that travels around and around underneath the parachute bringing forth the Ghost Rider. How fast can you get the Ghost Rider to rocket?

Lead-Ins: Popcorn, Big Bang, Cat and Mouse, Shark, Rabbit and Hound.

Developmental Skills: Primary—cooperation, verbal contact, skillfulness and coordination; Secondary—adaptability, self-control, visual ability, reaction, strength.

Duration of Game: A few minutes.

Appropriate Ages: Under 6's might find this a big challenge.

When to Play: Middle.

Follow-Ups: Ball Surfing, Alligator, Popovers, Parachute Volleyball, Dodge 'em.

Gophers

Gophers

Spread the parachute out on the ground. All the players kneel around the edge of the parachute holding on to it except for a few gardeners who stand outside the parachute. Each gardener has a foam rubber ball. The gardeners ask players on one section of the parachute to burrow under the parachute to the other side and back. While the gophers are crawling underneath the parachute, the gardeners try to hit them with a foam ball. If a gopher gets hit, he or she trades places with the gardener. The new gardeners ask a different pack of gophers to cross under for the next round. You might also allow those holding on to the parachute to throw a ball if it comes to them.

Lead-Ins: Racing Heartbeat, Top of the Pops, Dodge 'em, Wave Wall, Raceway.

Developmental Skills: Primary—visual ability, reaction, crawling, throwing and catching, skillfulness and coordination, self-control, adaptability; Secondary—tactile contact, spontaneity.

Additional Equipment: Three to five foam balls.

When to Play: Middle.

Where to Play: On a soft surface, excluding dirt.

Follow-Ups: Sculpture, Centipede, Turnover, Treasure Hunt, Parachute Ride.

Heartbeat

Heartbeat

Here's how to create a nice, steady heartbeat. Everyone gets into a steady rhythm by making a mushroom, walking in a step or two and then walking back out as the parachute falls. When the blood has left the parachute, the players all lift up and step in to keep the heartbeat going.

Lead-Ins: Mushroom, Giant Mushroom, Wave Machine, Popcorn.

Developmental Skills: Primary—cooperation, adaptability, strength; Secondary—visual ability.

When to Play: Beginning.

Where to Play: Requires a tall ceiling.

Follow-Ups: Racing Heartbeat, Igloo, Floating Mushroom, other mushroom games.

It's in the Bag

Just because the parachute is all rolled up in the bag don't think that you are necessarily through playing with it. One time we were playing with a group of very aggressive kids. The play session was officially over but the players were not ready to stop playing. One of them expressed his frustration by running up and kicking the duffel bag that was holding the parachute.

It was not only a good release for him but looked like fun. The others wanted to try it. It didn't hurt the duffel bag or the parachute so we said, "Why not!" A line quickly formed, and we took turns loosely holding the bag while all the kids had a chance to run up and kick it. Everyone had a turn, we all felt better, and we were ready to get on with the next activity.

It's in the Bag

Lead-Ins: Parachute Ride, Drag Race, Parachute Pass, Free Play, Group Balance.

Number of Players: Fewer than 24.

Developmental Skills: Primary—skillfulness and coordination; Secondary—cooperation, self-control, creativity, pantomime, visual ability, running, jumping.

Additional Equipment: A durable bag to hold the parachute.

When to Play: Ending.

Follow-Ups: None—the parachute is in the bag.

Lift Off

Lift Off

Does your waterbed have a leak? Here's how to make an air mattress. First, have everyone stretch the parachute out flat on the ground. Then a volunteer lies down in the middle. (If no one comes forward, guess who gets to go!) Those holding the edge of the parachute should roll it up several times to prevent it from ripping. How far you roll the parachute depends on how big the parachute is and how heavy the volunteer is: With a big parachute or a big person, you need to roll the edge up farther to make the parachute smaller.

At a given signal, everyone lifts together, gently and slowly. (Remind all lifters to lift with their legs and keep their backs straight.) Sweet dreams, at least for a minute. It's fun for the sleeper if those on the edge walk together in a circle. Don't forget to lower the sleeper gently so as not to cause a very rude awakening.

Safety Considerations: Especially with younger children, it is wise to have four or more adults spread around the parachute to insure a soft landing for the sleeper.

Lead-Ins: Group Balance, Sculpture, Wave Rolling, Centipede, Turnover.

Number of Players: 12 or more.

Developmental Skills: Primary—trust, strength, cooperation; Secondary—verbal contact, self-control, visual ability.

Appropriate Ages: Players must be old enough and mature enough not to suddenly drop someone. We don't recommend this for players younger than 12 years of age.

When to Play: Middle.

Where to Play: Play this on a soft surface such as grass or mats—not on concrete.

Follow-Ups: Circular Tug, Circular Sit-Ups, Racing Heartbeat, Spin Out.

Missile Launch

10, 9, 8, 7, 6, 5, 4, 3, 2, 1 . . . Ignition . . . Liftoff! The bird has flown! To be honest, this game is not as dramatic as a real missile launch; but you do get to launch a missile, sort of. Four or five players, each one carrying a ball, go under the parachute. While mission control (those around the outside of the parachute) makes a mushroom, the missile launchers attempt to throw their balls through the hole in the center of the parachute. How many missiles can they launch in one mushroom? Be sure to give everyone a chance.

For a real challenge, ask the missile launchers to bounce their balls off the ground and through the hole.

Missile Launch

Safety Considerations: Use only soft foam balls.

Lead-Ins: Waves Overhead, Sculpture, Shark, any mushroom or popcorn games.

Developmental Skills: Primary—visual ability, throwing and catching, self-control, cooperation; Secondary—skillfulness and coordination, reaction, jumping.

Additional Equipment: Foam balls that fit through the hole in the center of the parachute.

Appropriate Ages: This may prove too great a challenge for the under 6's.

When to Play: Middle.

Follow-Ups: Dodge 'em, Treasure Hunt, Alligator, Centipede, any game.

Parachute Volleyball

Parachute Volleyball

If you are lucky enough to have two small parachutes (both 12 feet or less), you can play with them together. For this game you also need a ball, the bigger the better. Imagine how you would play volleyball. Each team has a parachute. The net is optional. It takes a lot of teamwork not to send the ball flying out of control. The idea is to get the ball over to the other parachute.

If you ever figure out a way to spike the ball please let us know, and send a photo!

Lead-Ins: Interlocking Gears, any mushroom or popcorn games.

Number of Players: 12 or more.

Developmental Skills: Primary—cooperation; Secondary—self-control, strength, problem solving, verbal contact, adaptability, visual ability.

Additional Equipment: Another parachute, a ball.

Appropriate Ages: May be too difficult for children under age 6.

When to Play: Middle.

Where to Play: Need enough room for two fully opened parachutes.

Follow-Ups: Interlocking Gears, Big Bang, or any popcorn and mushroom games.

Popovers

Popovers

Divide the players into two teams facing each other across an imaginary line bisecting the parachute. Pull the parachute taut and place half the balls close to the edge on one team's side, and the other half close to the edge on the opposite side. Each team tries to shake the parachute hard enough to make the balls pop over the heads of the other team. One suggestion for making this challenge more interesting is to assign point values to different colored balls. Let's say all the yellow balls count as one point and the red balls count as three. This should change the strategy a bit. Of course, once the game is over, who keeps track of the score?

Lead-Ins: Wave Machine, Popcorn, Big Bang, any of the games with balls.

Developmental Skills: Primary—cooperation, reaction; Secondary—verbal contact, self-control, spontaneity, visual ability, adaptability, strength, endurance.

Additional Equipment: Six balls, three one color and three another color.

Duration of Game: Game may go very quickly but can be replayed several times.

Appropriate Ages: Young children may be happy just to bounce the balls around.

When to Play: Middle.

Follow-Ups: Big Bang, Snake Tag, Gophers, Rabbit and Hound, other ball games.

Shark

Shark

Let's go to the beach! Players hold the parachute about waist high and stretched taut. One player, the shark, goes underneath the parachute with a Frisbee. The shark holds the edge of the Frisbee against the parachute while circling underneath to make it look as if a shark fin is rising up out of the water. The other players can make small waves with the parachute to simulate the ocean and hum the soundtrack from the movie, Jaws, "Dum-dum dum-dum dum-dum."

Watch out! The shark may decide to bite one of the players holding on to the edge of the parachute by grabbing a leg. This player then cries out, takes the Frisbee from the shark, and becomes the new shark. Warning: If there are enough Frisbees, a feeding frenzy might develop as more and more sharks enter the water!

Lead-Ins: Wave Machine, World Record Merry-Go-Round, any mushroom games.

Developmental Skills: Primary—tactile contact, spontaneity, pantomime, cooperation; Secondary—walking, verbal contact, adaptability, self-control, visual ability.

Additional Equipment: Three to five Frisbees.

When to Play: Middle.

Follow-Ups: Spin Out, Turnover, Drag Race, Parachute Ride, It's in the Bag.

Spin Out

Spin Out

Have three people sit down together in the middle of the parachute with their backs together facing out. They might want to interlock their arms.

These three players sit very still, and everyone else slowly walks around in a circle, wrapping the three up in the parachute. The players in the middle may want to use their hands to make sure the parachute doesn't wrap around their necks.

When the three are wrapped up to about chest level, it's time to give the spin-out signal. At the signal everyone quickly steps straight back at the same time while pulling on the parachute. This spins the people in the middle around quite fast for two or three revolutions, kind of like a homemade amusement ride.

Safety Considerations: Make absolutely sure that players in the middle don't get their necks wrapped up in the parachute.

Activity Level: Low/moderate.

Lead-Ins: Lift Off, Pony Express, Treasure Hunt, Missile Launch, Parachute Pass.

Developmental Skills: Primary—cooperation, tactile contact, strength; Secondary—reaction, walking, balancing.

When to Play: Middle.

Where to Play: This game can be played on the grass but you will get grass or dirt stains on the parachute. For maximum effect and minimum wear and tear on the parachute, we recommend playing this game on a slippery surface, such as a recently waxed, wooden gym floor.

Follow-Ups: Cop and Robber, Wave Rolling, Over Under, Drag Race, Parachute Ride.

Treasure Hunt

Throw everything under the parachute: balls, jump ropes, Frisbees, stale bread. Everything is fair game. Arrange all the players around the parachute and have them make a steady Heartbeat. On the up-swing point to one or more people to go under the parachute, search for a particular treasure, and bring it out. The Heartbeat gives an automatic time limit: If a seeker stays too long and gets touched by the parachute, she or he must rebury the treasure for the next round.

Safety Considerations: Remind players to watch out for collisions when racing to collect treasure.

Lead-Ins: Heartbeat, Rabbit and Hound, Pony Express, Rocking Chair, Snake Tag.

Developmental Skills: Primary—self-control, visual ability, skillfulness and coordination, reaction; Secondary—problem solving, running, cooperation, verbal contact, adaptability.

Additional Equipment: Balls, jump ropes, Frisbees, stale bread, any available small objects.

When to Play: Middle.

Follow-Ups: Racing Heartbeat, Popovers, Parachute Golf, Spin Out, Ostrich, Igloo.

Wave Machine

The easiest parachute game, and the one everyone plays without any prompting, is Wave Machine. Simply spread out the parachute, grab an edge, and begin to shake. Tiny ripples will soon turn into frothy waves.

Lead-In: Free Play.

Developmental Skills: Primary—strength, endurance; Secondary—cooperation, self-control.

When to Play: Beginning.

Follow-Ups: Popcorn games or a low activity level game to give players a rest.

Waves Overhead

Would the group like to give a great gift to a couple of players? Send three to five scuba divers in to lie down under the parachute while the rest of the players vigorously shake the parachute. This makes strong waves over the divers. It's a great way to cool off on a hot day.

Lead-Ins: Heartbeat, Racing Heartbeat, Dodge 'em, Jelly-fish Jaunt, Raceway.

Developmental Skills: Primary—strength, endurance; Secondary—cooperation, self-control, tactile contact.

When to Play: Middle.

Follow-Ups: Centipede, Cop and Robber, Flying Parachute, Spin Out, Cat and Mouse.

High Activity
Parachute Games

Playing with a parachute is a pretty exciting experience, and here are 15 of the most exciting high activity games. If attention is beginning to wane, try one of these!

Cat and Mouse

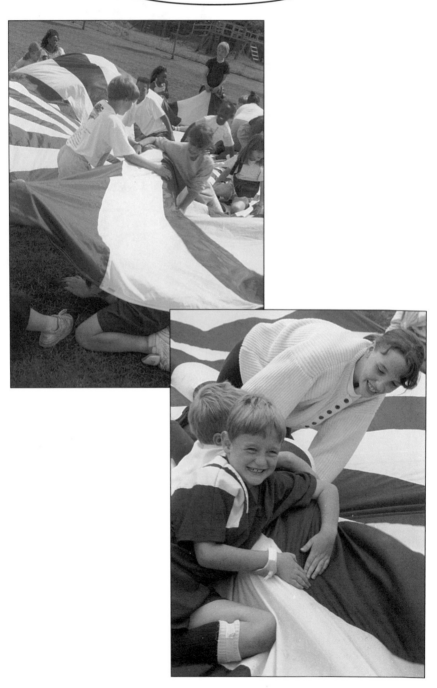

Cat and Mouse

Cats chase mice. To protect themselves the mice in this game hide under the parachute. Everyone holds the parachute loosely at about waist level. Whoever has a birthday closest to June 9 (or any date you prefer) gets to be under the parachute as the mouse. The player wearing the most yellow gets on top of the parachute as the cat.

The cat closes its eyes while everyone begins making waves to help hide the mouse. The mouse stays low and scurries underneath the parachute to avoid the cat. The cat, who is on all four paws, opens its eyes and tries to catch the mouse underneath all the waves. Usually the cat has a time limit with everyone counting out loud in unison to 20 or some other appropriate number. The cat and mouse then choose someone who hasn't gone before to play out the next round.

Depending on the size (i.e., age) and number of your players you might want to experiment with different numbers of cats and mice. A strategy tip: Players can either use the parachute to help the mouse escape from the cat or to reveal the mouse to the cat by holding the parachute down momentarily. Please play fair with this tip.

Safety Considerations: Avoid playing on concrete or blacktop. Cats and mice may suffer scrapes and bruises, and the hard surface may tear the parachute.

Lead-Ins: Racing Heartbeat, Free Play, most low or moderate activity games.

Developmental Skills: Primary—cooperation, tactile contact, visual ability, reaction, leaning, crawling; Secondary—verbal contact, self-control, spontaneity, strength, endurance.

Duration of Game: This game could go on until everyone gets a turn being a cat or mouse.

When to Play: Middle.

Where to Play: Best played on a soft surface such as mats. Can be played on grass, if you don't mind grass stains on everyone's clothing and the parachute.

Follow-Ups: Any low or moderate activity game such as Circular Sit-Ups.

Flying Parachute

Flying Parachute

Have everyone gather at the edge of one half of the parachute and hold the edge with one hand. Everyone takes off running in the same direction. This gives the impression of trying to launch a giant wounded kite.

Safety Considerations: Remind players to watch where they're going! Sometimes they get so caught up in the excitement, they forget to watch out for holes, water sprinklers, and other low-altitude hazards.

Lead-Ins: Group Balance, Igloo, Blow Up, Turnover, Ostrich, Big Bang.

Number of Players: 24 or fewer.

Developmental Skills: Primary—cooperation, reaction, endurance, running; Secondary—verbal contact, adaptability, self-control, visual ability, strength.

When to Play: Middle.

Where to Play: Find a place that has enough space to make a good run.

Follow-Ups: Lift Off, Parachute Pass, Who's Peeking?, Missile Launch, Free Play.

Housekeeping

Housekeeping

A team of three or four players stands a bit away from the parachute. This is the neatness team. Their job is to make sure that all the balls stay on the parachute. Meanwhile, the messy team is trying to shake all the balls off the parachute. At the end of 30 seconds or so everyone stops to tally up how many balls are on the parachute and how many are off. Select a new neatness team and repeat until everyone has had a turn to be neat.

Lead-Ins: Wave Machine, Popcorn, Snake Tag, Ostrich, or any less active game.

Developmental Skills: Primary—cooperation, adaptability, self-control, visual ability, strength, throwing and catching; Secondary—problem solving, verbal contact, spontaneity, endurance, running.

Additional Equipment: At least more foam balls than the number of players on the neatness team.

When to Play: Middle.

Follow-Ups: Basketball, Pony Express, Waves Overhead, Cat and Mouse.

I Dare Ya

I Dare Ya

Two teams—every other person—are evenly spread out around the parachute. Both teams make steady heartbeats together. The teams take turns challenging each other to complete some goal before a set number of heartbeat pulses. The challenge can be fulfilled underneath, around, or completely away from the parachute.

For example, one dare might be for each team member to touch his or her toes in one pulse. Easy. A different challenge could be for everyone to touch a door and come back to the parachute in two pulses.

A dare does not have to involve the entire team. One hero representing the team might be challenged to do 10 push-ups in two pulses. Or the goal could require that the entire team work together, perhaps forming a line long enough to have someone touch a tree while the other end holds on to the parachute in three heartbeats.

Be careful not to make too tough of a challenge. The other team has the option to contest the dare. This means that for honor to be fulfilled the challenging team must be able to perform the feat.

Safety Considerations: No dare should be truly dangerous.

Lead-Ins: Heartbeat, any mushroom game, any low or moderate activity game.

Developmental Skills: Primary— reaction, endurance, self-control; Secondary—cooperation, verbal contact, tactile contact, creativity, visual ability, skillfulness and coordination, running, hopping, problem solving, adaptability, spontaneity.

When to Play: Middle.

Where to Play: Best to have some space around the parachute for more dare possibilities.

Follow-Ups: Treasure Hunt, Turnover, Spin Out, or any less active game.

Jell-O

Everyone crawls underneath the parachute except for a couple of cooks who remain outside. These cooks want to make People Jell-O. They ask the ingredients to move or raise certain body parts to make forms under the parachute. For instance, a cook might call out, "Three jumping jacks" or "Lie on your back and raise your left leg straight up." If a cook chooses to taste the creation, he or she changes places with someone under the parachute.

Lead-Ins: Racing Heartbeat, Sculpture, Cop and Robber, Floating Mushroom, Shark.

Developmental Skills: Primary—visual ability, crawling; Secondary—cooperation, verbal contact, tactile contact, creativity, pantomime, skillfulness and coordination, jumping, hopping.

When to Play: Middle.

Follow-Ups: Basketball, Climb the Mountain, Gophers, Wave Rolling.

Jellyfish Jaunt

One day a group of players asked if they could take a run with the parachute. Well, why not? Everyone gathered around the parachute and took off. It looked like the world's largest multicolored jellyfish had been let loose in the park. Could this be the subject for the next Stephen King novel?

Safety Considerations: Players need to watch for anyone who happens to fall. In fact, the jellyfish should avoid passing too closely to or running over any object because the following side might not see the object and get into a real jam! As always when running, be aware of holes, sprinkler heads and so on.

Lead-Ins: Sculpture, Turnover, Blow Up, any low activity games.

Number of Players: 12 or more.

Developmental Skills: Primary—endurance, running; Secondary—cooperation, verbal contact, adaptability, spontaneity, self-control, visual ability.

When to Play: Middle.

Where to Play: Give yourself enough space for a decent run.

Follow-Ups: Free Play, Ostrich, Who's Peeking?, Cover Up, any low activity games.

Merry-Go-Round

Merry-Go-Round

Merry-Go-Round

This game brings back the spirit of the old carousels. Everyone grabs an edge of the parachute with one hand and begins walking in a giant circle. To really get into the mood you can start bobbing up and down as you walk, just like the wooden horses.

Got the idea? Have everyone run a lap, then jump on both feet for a lap. How about hopping on one foot? Or alternate, five hops on the left foot, five on the right. Can you all skip together while holding the parachute? How about a gallop? After a while, switch directions.

Lead-Ins: Flying Parachute, Jellyfish Jaunt, any lower activity game.

Developmental Skills: Primary—walking, jumping, hopping; Secondary—cooperation, skillfulness and coordination, endurance, verbal contact, adaptability, self-control, balancing.

When to Play: Middle.

Follow-Ups: World Record Merry-Go-Round, any lower activity game.

Pony Express

Pony Express

Players pair up: One person goes under the parachute while the teammate stands outside. The player underneath sits or crouches under the parachute facing out and is the rider. The outside player faces in, holds on to the parachute, and is the pony. All the ponies lift the parachute up. This releases the riders who crawl between their ponies' legs and run around the parachute. While the riders are running, the ponies make a mushroom and get down on all fours bringing the parachute with them. It's similar to Climb the Mountain, except the players keep holding on to the parachute with their hands instead of tucking it under their knees. The riders come back to mount the horses who are all set to cross the great big mountain of parachute before them. Switch roles and repeat.

Safety Considerations: It's a good idea to pair players of similar size so that one doesn't get squished. Remind riders that the saddle is back on the pony's hips, not on their poor pony's back.

Pony Express

Lead-Ins: Cat and Mouse, Climb the Mountain, Igloo, Rocking Chair, Centipede.

Developmental Skills: Primary—tactile contact, skillfulness and coordination, leaning, crawling; Secondary—cooperation, verbal contact, self-control, visual ability, reaction, balancing.

When to Play: Middle.

Where to Play: A soft surface is best.

Follow-Ups: Treasure Hunt, Waves Overhead, Cop and Robber, Gophers, Shark.

Popcorn

Popcorn

If you have lots of soft balls you can make a giant popcorn machine. Just throw the light, spongy balls on the parachute. People will get the idea.

Activity Level: Moderate/high.

Lead-Ins: Wave Machine, Shark, mushroom and low activity games.

Developmental Skills: Primary—endurance; Secondary—self-control, spontaneity, visual ability, reaction, strength, throwing and catching.

Additional Equipment: At least three (or as many as you have) foam balls or other soft, bouncy objects.

When to Play: Beginning.

Follow-Ups: Mushroom, Jellyfish Jaunt, any moderate or low activity games.

Raceway

This is good training for rush hour traffic. Everyone holds on to the parachute and walks in a circle as in Merry-Go-Round. The leader calls out different instructions and explains who is to do what. For example, all left handers might be asked to pass two drivers in front of them. The left-handed players would then let go of the parachute and try to pass the two right-handed (obviously) people in front of them who are still holding on to the parachute. The object of the game is to get to the head of the circle. Just like driving on a raceway.

For a real workout, have players jog while they are holding the parachute. For more variety, have players switch directions.

Safety Considerations: Choose an area free from obstacles so the racers can run safely.

Lead-Ins: Cover Up, Free Play, Circular Tug, Swooping Cloud, mushroom games.

Developmental Skills: Primary—endurance, running, Secondary—adaptability, self-control, visual ability, verbal contact.

When to Play: Middle.

Follow-Ups: Ghost Rider, Group Balance, Parachute Pass, Turnover, Drag Race.

Racing Heartbeat

Racing Heartbeat

Once you establish a heartbeat, you can have people cross under the parachute while it is in the air. Be careful! Everyone will want to run under the parachute at the same time. To prevent total pandemonium you should take time to explain the activity first, clarify that everyone will get a chance to cross under, and state that specific categories of who should cross will be announced.

For instance, as the parachute is going up, ask people who are wearing certain types or colors of clothes to cross under the parachute. Or you can select players by their birth month. Another category is according to favorite flavor of ice cream: strawberry, chocolate, or vanilla. Or you could find out who has a cat by seeing who crosses under when you call out, "All those with cats!" Or who prefers history to mathematics. For a big surprise call out any all-inclusive category, such as all those born between January 1 and December 31.

Racing Heartbeat

Safety Considerations: Be sure to remind players to watch out for others as they run underneath the parachute. (Everyone tends to converge in the middle.) Elderly or physically fragile people should consider the potential for jarring contact.

Warning: Sometimes parachute hearts can develop arrhythmia. This happens when people mistakenly think the object of the game is to bring the parachute down quickly on one of the runners. Unfortunately this strategy can lower the edge of the parachute down to the same level as someone's neck who is running fairly fast. (The Surgeon General has determined that running into a parachute edge and not under it may be harmful to the neck!) It is important to stress to the players that the parachute must maintain a steady speed.

Lead-Ins: Heartbeat, Mushroom, Jumbo Mushroom, low activity games.

Developmental Skills: Primary—cooperation, trust, adaptability, visual ability, strength; Secondary—verbal contact, tactile contact, self-control, creativity, running.

When to Play: Middle.

Follow-Ups: Floating Parachute, Over Under, Flying Parachute, low activity games.

Snake Tag

Snake Tag

Throw a bunch of short ropes on the parachute. Divide the parachute down the middle into two opposing teams. The object is to shake the parachute so vigorously that a snake bites someone on the other team. Watch out that you don't get bitten yourself!

You may find that young children simply enjoy making the ropes bounce.

Safety Considerations: Jump ropes work well if they don't have heavy, dangerous handles.

Activity Level: Moderate/high but should maintain its steady pulse.

Lead-Ins: Wave Machine, Popcorn, Big Bang, Popovers, any games with balls.

Developmental Skills: Primary—strength; Secondary—adaptability, self-control, visual ability, reaction, endurance.

Additional Equipment: Ropes that measure 4 to 6 feet.

When to Play: Middle.

Follow-Ups: A somewhat lower activity game, such as Blow Up.

Top of the Pops

Top of the Pops

One group of players spontaneously started to play this game. We liked it so we are including it here. The game is Popcorn with people added on top of the parachute. The three or four people who are on the parachute try to throw the bouncing balls off. Popcorn poppers, those who are around the edge of the parachute, try to keep the popcorn in the popper. In other words, they retrieve the balls and toss them back on the parachute. Just for fun, you can yell "Freeze!" at some point, say after playing for a minute or two, and see how many balls of popcorn are on and how many are off the parachute.

Safety Considerations: It's best not to use hard or even inflated balls. Somebody inevitably ends up getting whacked in the head.

Lead-Ins: Popcorn, Big Bang, Parachute Volleyball, any less active game.

Developmental Skills: Primary—throwing and catching, self-control, visual ability, reaction, strength, crawling; Secondary—tactile contact, endurance, spontaneity, skillfulness and coordination.

Additional Equipment: Four or five foam balls (any other kind might roll away too far).

When to Play: Middle.

Follow-Ups: Snake Tag, popcorn games, any less active game.

Wave Rolling

Wave Rolling

After people see the parachute as a Wave Machine, many want to get on top. So, let them. For the best all-around experience, limit the number of players on the parachute to five. Everyone around the edge gets to make waves. With too many on the parachute or too few wave makers it looks as if you are sailing through the doldrums.

Once the storm begins, you will find out how seaworthy people are as they crawl and roll around on the waves.

Safety Considerations: Ask those on the waves to get on their hands and knees. Waves are difficult to walk on without falling, especially on a hard surface. You may also want players on the waves to remove their shoes for each other's and the parachute's safety.

Activity Level: Moderate/high.

Lead-Ins: Wave Machine, Spin Out, Rabbit and Hound, Popcorn, Parachute Golf.

Developmental Skills: Primary—crawling, endurance, strength, trust, adaptability; Secondary—self-control, creativity, tactile contact, visual ability, problem solving, spontaneity.

When to Play: Middle.

Where to Play: Best played on a soft surface such as grass, carpeting, or mats.

Follow-Ups: Top of the Pops, Snake Tag, Popovers, Pony Express, Cat and Mouse.

World Record Merry-Go-Round

Set a Frisbee or some other marker on the ground outside but near the parachute and you can play a competitive version of Merry-Go-Round. What is interesting is that the group ends up competing against itself.

Use a stop watch to time how long it takes the players to make one complete revolution clockwise, stop, and then return to the same starting position by going counterclockwise. Now, can we beat that record?

 Safety Considerations: Make sure players watch out for little ones in a mixed-age group. Sometimes they fall and risk getting trodden on or fall while holding on to the parachute in which case they may get dragged.

────── World Record Merry-Go-Round ──────

Lead-Ins: Merry-Go-Round, Cover Up, Group Balance, Blow Up, Ostrich, Igloo.

Developmental Skills: Primary—running, jumping, hopping; Secondary—cooperation, endurance, verbal contact, adaptability, self-control, skillfulness and coordination, reaction, balancing.

Additional Equipment: A Frisbee or some other marker.

When to Play: Middle.

Follow-Ups: Parachute Pass, Who's Peeking?, Drag Race, any lower activity game.

About the Authors

Todd Strong

Dale LeFevre

Todd Strong worked as lead trainer for the New Games Foundation, a nonprofit organization that teaches personal and professional development by bringing people closer together through play. In this position, he traveled throughout the United States conducting workshops, during which he was able to collect and try out parachute games in many settings and with different populations. When he became the Foundation's program director, his responsibilities included planning and promoting New Games and New Games Workshops worldwide. A past director and current active member of the International Jugglers Association, Todd has authored many books on juggling, including *The Devil Stick Book*, *The Diablo Book*, and *Diablo for Advanced Players*. He taught juggling in Germany for four years and is currently Professeur de Jonglerie at the national circus school of France in Rosny-sous-Bois. Todd earned his bachelor's degree in recreation from California State University at Hayward and his master's in experiential education from Mankato State University in Minnesota.

Dale LeFevre has over 20 years of experience presenting, collecting, and perfecting games for parachutes. He started his career as a trainer for the New Games Foundation in 1975 and by 1976 was associate director. In 1977 he started his own project, Play Express, which took New Games into schools in more than 30 countries around the world. Dale is the author of the popular book *New Games for the Whole Family*.

The director of New Games International, Dale works with companies through his new venture, Playworks, where New Games are used in the workplace to improve communication and teamwork and to reduce stress.

Dale received a bachelor's degree in business from Valparaiso University in Indiana and a master's in education from New York University.

Parachute Games
Todd Strong and Dale LeFevre

Also by the authors:

Todd Strong: *The Devil Stick Book*, *The Diablo Book*, *Diablo for Advanced Players*, *Diablo Postcards*, *The Dice Stacking Book*

Dale LeFevre: *New Games for the Whole Family*
Videos: The New Games Video, New Games From Around the World, New Soccer (For Fun and Skills), Rainy Day Games (You Can Make), Sunny Day Games (You Can Make)

Contact addresses:
Todd Strong
École National de Cirque de Rosny
Stade Pierre Letessier
Rue Jules Guesde
93110 Rosny-sous-Bois, France

Dale LeFevre
P.O. Box 1641
Mendocino, CA 95460
707-937-3337

Dale LeFevre offers New Games Workshops for professional and personal development, enabling participants to expand their creativity and develop leadership skills. At a New Games Workshop you will learn how to facilitate creative play, integrate cooperation and competition, use New Games in your program or classroom, and adapt games so that everyone can play them. Who should attend? Recreation leaders, teachers, community organizers, personnel directors, social workers, camp directors, and parents can all benefit enormously from New Games Workshops. To arrange or attend a New Games Workshop, contact Dale LeFevre, the director, at the above address or phone number.

"Look at the faces of these people: They're smiling! This is the most exciting development in physical education in 50 years!"

Seymour M. Gold, University of California at Davis

*You'll find
other outstanding
physical education
resources at*

www.humankinetics.com

In the U.S. call
1-800-747-4457

Australia ....(08) 8277-1555
Canada..............................(800) 465-7301
Europe .... +44 (0) 113-278-1708
New Zealand ....(09) 309-1890

HUMAN KINETICS
The Information Leader in Physical Activity
P.O. Box 5076 • Champaign, IL 61825-5076 USA